GATHER TOGETHER, FELLOW WOMEN

GATHER TOGETHER, FELLOW WOMEN

JALIA KANGAVE

WITH ANNETTE TUSH

To our mothers and to the loving memory of our grandmothers.
To all the women who came before us.
Thank you for making it possible for us to enjoy the liberties that we enjoy today.

The names of some individuals have been changed to protect their privacy.

Acknowledgments

IF YOU ARE LOOKING for someone who is going to meticulously comb through your book, ask you questions that make you dig deeper into your story and reflect on some of her own personal experiences to make you feel connected, then you should work with our copy editor, Jane Belton. She's awesome. We would not have been encouraged to write this book were it not for the numerous and varied reactions from our Facebook community. Some of you came into our inboxes and opened up about your very personal experiences. Others shared our posts. And others told us to "go ahead and write the book". And, without a doubt, our lives have been immeasurably enriched by all the phenomenal women that we are blessed to call our mothers, sisters and friends. To all of you, we are deeply grateful.

"Women give birth with other women."

~ Alur proverb

CONTENTS

Poems

GATHER TOGETHER

"When the webs of the spider join, they can trap a lion."
~ Amhara proverb

I AM IMMENSELY BLESSED.
Every single day, I get to speak with at least one of my seven siblings. My mother's love, even during moments when we disagree, has never been questionable. My father has never told me that he loves me. And many times, we don't see eye to eye. And yet, I know that in his own way, he loves me dearly. My daughters – at just six and seven years old – boldly call me out for my inconsistencies and love me even during times when I feel unlovable. I am married to a man who is never threated by my achievements and who I commune with for hours on end.

I am blessed with the women in my life. My biological sisters. My girlfriends from high school. The girlfriends that I made through work and through my travels. The women of Barnett Road, where I live. All of them inspire me, challenge me, cry with me, make me laugh, counsel me and cheer me on. Their playfulness reminds me not to take life too seriously. Their vulnerability gives me permission to be gentle with myself and has enabled me to forgive myself for things that I once thought unforgiveable. I have also been blessed by the words of female artists. Maya Angelou. India Arie. Erykah Badu. Tracy Chapman. Their generosity in sharing some of the most intimate details of their lives and challenging reductionist perceptions of womanhood, have on the one hand been a soothing balm and on the other hand emboldened me to share my own experiences.

I am blessed to live on Barnett Road. Where I can knock on a neighbour's door to ask for two tablespoons of turmeric when, in the middle of making a curry, I realize that I have run out of spice. A neighbourhood where my husband and Terry, our neighbour, decided to jointly buy a lawnmower because it did not make sense to have two lawnmowers for two households. Rebecca brings bath bombs for our daughters because she "thinks that the girls will love them" (also probably because the girls accost her with home-made cards soaked in love hearts). The other day, Sue and Steve brought a doll cot that they had owned for over twenty years. Tucked sweetly under the delicately ironed quilt was a black doll dressed in red and gold satin and a white doll dressed in a red knitted outfit, two tiny books gently located at their feet. Steve had painted it lush pink earlier in the week and tightened the screws that morning. Sue wanted it to go to a home where it would be treasured. It sits right beside our daughters' bunk bed. And even though Emma, Stephen and Trudy (the dog) recently left Barnett Road, our girls still consider Trudy one of their best friends. They cried inconsolably when they found out that she would be leaving.

I feel blessed to have finally come to the realization that God loves me in spite of my imperfections. That God remains compassionate even when I fall short and fall back. That all is well in God's timing.

I have also been blessed to know pain. A reminder of my humanness. The pain of being told, as a young girl, that I was not beautiful – a burden that I silently and arduously carried through my teenage years and which stung for a significant part of my adult life. The pain of betrayal by those that I entrusted with my innocence, my youth and my fragile heart. The pain of a miscarriage. The pain of walking through life not feeling like I was worthy. Battles with insecurity. And the suffering that comes from envy and fear and comparison.

The greatest source of my wounds has not always been from bruises acquired from grave adversities. Rather, it has often been in the subtle trespasses of everyday living, largely born out of comparison with the lives of others. My inability to measure up to the glossy images that I see on television and social media. The stories that I have told myself about what people must be thinking of me. The fears surrounding milestones relating to my children. *Should I be worried that they are not walking by their first birthday when Sonia's mother said that both her children were walking by nine months old? Will they ever get out of nappies? Should I still celebrate my children after finding out that some of their peers got "above expected" for all areas in their report cards, when ours had some "expected"? Are they reading books in the book band expected of children their age? What about swimming and gymnastics levels? Am I a good mother? Will my husband leave me like my friend's husband left her? What am I going to do about those naughty seven kilograms that have taken occupancy around my waist and my thighs and show no sign of migrating? Does my boss think less of me because I do not publish as many papers as my peers? Will people still think that I am intelligent when they get to know that I quit a prestigious career in academia to dedicate more time to my daughters and to pursue my desire to write? Can I even call myself a writer?*

The list continues.

These daily trespasses and casual brushes with not enough-ness create a chronic sense of lack. They breed immense suffering. All of a sudden, in comparison with others, my life becomes WORTH LESS. I become LESS THAN. And all of my achievements become meaningless in comparison with the big bangs of others.

The circles of women in my life help me gain better perspective. The countless hours spent on the phone with my soul sister, Nuruh, unpicking uncomfortable emotions, remind me of the things that truly matter. It is in sitting under the gaze of a dim light in a warmly heated living room, on a winter night, sipping on cardamom tea and nibbling on home-baked coffee cake with the women of Barnett Road, that my mind refocuses on the gifts of womanhood. We get to share the "expression of our souls – in whichever form that takes" as my dear friend Sheila, so beautifully put it. It is in gathering on a colourful sisal handwoven mat with Neema, Aisha, Sophia and Rosemary in the compound of Farida's parents, following the death of her father, that I experience the gifts of sisterhood. Other times, the saving grace comes in the form of a mum-friend who is brave enough to constantly ask for help with school drop-offs and pick-ups in an environment where we have been led to believe that asking for help is a sign of weakness and self-sufficiency is the embodiment of strength.

Our shared womanhood means that we are able to recognize ourselves in each other, often without the need to explain ourselves. Whether we are black or white or brown. Married, divorced or single. Thin or fat. Religious or agnostic.

I never considered myself a feminist until quite recently. Growing up in a household where our mother gave both her daughters and her sons equal opportunities and shared responsibilities, it didn't occur to me that I needed extra layers of support as a girl and, later, as a woman. I was quite disturbed, for example, when I found out that girls in Uganda were given an extra 1.5 points to help them gain entry into university. I recall secretly frowning on this affirmative action. I thought to myself: why do they think we need special treatment? Do they think that we are not as intelligent as the boys? This was obviously invigorated by the lyrics of Destiny's Child's "Independent Women": "I buy my own diamonds and I buy my own rings … Cause I depend on me if I want it."

In law school, I deliberately stayed away from courses such as Gender and the Law. I did not want to be labelled an angry woman. Neither did I perceive myself as a woman in need of salvation. After law school, I steered clear of fields of law that were dominated by women. Family Law. Human Rights Law. Health and the Law. I chose a career in Tax Law.

This is not to say that I did not understand that there were girls and women who, for various reasons, were marginalized. Rather, I did not see myself in them.

And then I got married.

It is one thing to grow up in the era of "Independent Women" and quite another to navigate the complex terrain of marriage. No amount of education really prepares you for the extent to which patriarchy is entrenched in society and perhaps, even, in our own minds. And when you grow up in a society where marriage is the ultimate goal, you internalize a set of rules that you need to play by if you are to keep your marriage. People don't necessarily walk up to you and say that you need to do this or that or the other for you to stay married. But you learn, over time, that there are certain things that society expects of a good wife. I had been an observant student. I had noted that a good wife went back home straight after work to ensure that dinner was ready, before having a shower and changing into her newest acquisition of Victoria's Secret lingerie. Meanwhile, her husband of three months and his friends took a detour to Kampala's Africana Hotel for tea and samosas from 5.30pm to 10pm, Monday to Friday. A good wife did not ask her husband why he habitually came home after midnight, but she sent him a text message to let him know where she would be on the odd occasion when she would hang out with colleagues after work. A good wife did not raise her concerns about the toll that housework and childcare were having on her because she did not want to rock the boat. She rarely voiced the things that she was dissatisfied with because to do so would amount to nagging. And nagging could have severe consequences. I had witnessed how those who did not conform to these rules of engagement were punished. Silent treatment. Silencing. Blaming. Shaming. Divorce. Ridicule.

And so, when I got married, despite the fact that my husband and I both worked full time, somehow, at the end of the day, I had to figure out what we were going to have for dinner, who was going to pick our daughters from nursery, what time they were going to bed and how to occupy them over the weekends. Along with my crammed work diary, I was occupied with thoughts about the dirty laundry that was piling up, the dishes that would spend the night in the sink, playdates that would need to be arranged, dentist appointments that needed to be scheduled and what we would have for breakfast the next morning. Meanwhile, ringing loudly and constantly in my head were sirens warning me of the threat of my husband leaving me if I did not "give" him sex at the end of a very exhausting day. After all, there was sufficient data – stories of women who had been left or cheated on because they failed to perform acrobatics in bed. Forget about being tired. Your primary goal was to satisfy your man.

I was chronically exhausted. And I started feeling resentful. The generous smile that had been my trademark for several years had been replaced with a stretched and sometimes angry look. And yet, I did not want to rock the boat. I did not want my husband to think of me as a quarrelsome woman. I lived in fear of being left. So, for the most part, I suffered in silence.

All of this made me wonder: *If I can have such a difficult time navigating these waters when I am educated, financially independent and married to a progressive man, what are the options for a woman who does not have an education and who depends on a man for subsistence? What are the options for a woman who is in an abusive relationship and feels that she has nowhere to report? What are the options for the woman whose immigration status depends entirely on her relationship with the man in question?*

Marriage turned me into a feminist. I realized that I was going to have to devise means to save myself. However, I would need to rely on the wisdom of a village of women. I was going to have to learn how to communicate my needs and put aside the unrealistic and unachievable expectations deposited on women. I was going to have to trust that the man that I was married to was intelligent enough, reasonable enough and compassionate enough. I was going to have to let go of the fear of being abandoned and the obsession with wanting to prove to him that I am, indeed, a good woman. I was going to have to stop feeling that I needed to be "doing" all the time. To stop relentlessly trying to patch up moments of silence and to allow myself to just be.

What I needed to do was to relax, breathe and put down the baggage that I had been carrying around for so many years. Baggage that had made me shrink; sometimes even disappear.

Much of what I write about in this book is a collection of musings that I have written over a period of three years. I write this book not because I have answers, but because I am a seeker, paddling through the journey of life. Indeed, I find that I have more questions than I do answers. I have often gained much comfort, strength and wisdom from poems, books and songs written and performed by women over decades. This is my offering. My sister-friend, Annette, has also contributed a chapter on grief, a wound to which only those who have experienced unimaginable loss can administer Band Aid. I hope that in our seeking, we add to the offering laid down by women who have come before us, those who walk alongside us and those who will follow in our footsteps.

THE NEST

"Ngu obusasi nibumanya akakumu"
"It is the hurt finger that knows best how much it pains."
~ *Runyankore proverb*

I WASN'T REALLY ENTHUSIASTIC when Sheila suggested that we should get together for a women's evening with a few other women on Barnett Road. I said yes because it seemed like the polite thing to say. We had been living on the road for close to two years. I could not keep turning down invitations, using my daughters as the excuse. But there was also a part of me that desperately missed being immersed in the company of women. I missed my sisters who, while living in the same country, were still miles away. We only got to see each other two or three times in a year. I missed my girlfriends in Kampala and the evenings that we used to spend at the Kampala Sheraton Hotel sipping on ginger spiced African tea accompanied by black forest cake, topped with whipped cream and cherries. There was always so much to talk about. Our high school days. Mean bosses. Quarrelsome neighbours. New relationships. Broken relationships. Births and deaths. I missed those nights in Vancouver when my sister-friend Annette and I would talk deep into the night about our dreams and aspirations. And the long walks with my sister-friend Shiva, around the University of British Columbia's Arcadia Park housing, voicing our concerns and frustrations with graduate school, or sitting around her dining table nibbling on pistachio nuts, mapping out grand plans for our post PhD life.

Maybe attending this women's gathering was not such a bad thing after all.

Yet, when the day came, I regretted saying yes. I was hit by the same wave of guilt that often hit me when I had to leave my daughters behind. Until that evening, I had never left our children with anyone other than my husband (excluding our visits to family in Uganda, where I happily left them with their grandparents or my siblings). I wondered what my husband would think of me leaving our girls with a babysitter to go out for a women's gathering. Would that make me appear reckless? Not a good mother? Leaving our precious children behind with a stranger for something that was not even an emergency? I myself had not always thought highly of women who left their children with strangers to go for a night out – even though technically the strangers were not really strangers (because they had been recommended by someone that the parents knew and trusted). To be honest, I had also come to relish my nights of solitude. Those quiet and peaceful nights after two chaotic little girls had finally retired to bed. The last thing I cared about was stepping out into the gloom of a chilly autumn night when I could be curled up in bed with a mug of hot chocolate, rereading Maya Angelou's *I Know Why the Caged Bird Sings* or delicately nibbling on Kahlil Gibran's *The Prophet.*

I went anyway.

And it turned out to be one of the best decisions that I have made in my life. As we sat around the dining table, breaking bread and sharing stories, then moving to the fireplace with our cups of Bosnian tea and orange cardamom cake, I was mesmerized by the raw openness of these women that I hardly knew and amazed by the compassion with which they listened to and held each other's stories. I knew then that I had found a home away from home. I got back home after midnight, feeling a wild yet gentle fire burning inside me. Unbeknown to me at the time, I was beginning a new chapter in my life. A new kind of woman was being birthed. A woman who was learning that there was no need for me to act strong when I was feeling burdened. That I did not have to beat myself up over the mistakes that I had made in the past, or even the ones that I was bound to make in the future. That perfection was an illusion and that it was okay not to be okay.

In the twelve or thirteen gatherings that we have collectively had since that autumn evening in 2017, Sheila, Zelah, Sue, Nergis and Janice have personified for me what it truly means to be human. Their ability to sit in pain and come out gentle on the other side. The courage to admit "I am hurting. I need help" or "I am exhausted. I do not have the emotional bandwidth to get together at this point in time" or "I am struggling". But also, "I am excited about the future" or "I feel absolutely fabulous right now" or "I am determined to do this, even though it feels a little scary." These women are educators, activists and health professionals. They are mothers, daughters and grandmothers. They run 10ks, make scrumptious curries and swim in seas in the winter. They are married and divorced and widowed. They bake cakes that could win *The Great British Bake Off*, carve sculptures out of stone, sew clothes that can be featured on runways and prune huge branches in their back gardens. They are vegetarians and meat eaters. They model not just womanhood but humanhood. They are a picture of life's pleasures and its pains. Its victories and its struggles. Its intelligence and its beauty. Its wisdom and its playfulness.

I would not have imagined that me, a Black woman, born in Uganda in the 1970s, raised in a Muslim family, would find kindred spirits in white and brown women, born in the United Kingdom and Pakistan in the 1960s, 1950s and 1940s and raised in Christian, Jewish, Muslim and agnostic families. That we could speak different languages and yet share the language of love and compassion. My poor imagination goes to show how quickly we forget the thick and unbreakable bond of our humanness. Through these women, I have witnessed what grace looks like and gained a deep appreciation for the sanctity and necessity of women's circles. Spaces where women feel free to express themselves without the fear of being judged and where shaming is exiled. Circles where there is no need to compete or show off about whose children are doing better, who has a more lucrative job, the most loving husband or the best kept home. Nests in which dreams are planted, victories celebrated, and struggles shared.

The Banyankole of Uganda have a saying: "It is the hurt finger that knows best how much it pains." Sometimes, however, this hurt finger tends to forget the pain. There are several ways – subtle and not so subtle – in which this amnesia manifests itself:

"I don't know how she can live in such a relationship. I would have walked out a long time ago."

"*Guma* (be strong). Other women have gone through worse things."

"Oh, you are pregnant? Again?!"

"Did you see how her son acted out in the playground? My children would never get away with such behaviour!"

"You are leaving your job to take care of your children? That's cute!"

"You are going back to work already (after the birth of a child)? You are a strong woman!"

"You are still breastfeeding that child?"

"You mean you did not breastfeed for the whole six months?"

"I am not surprised that her son turned out that way. That's what you get when you put work over your children."

"Your child is still in nappies?!"

"Am not surprised that he cheated on her. She brought it on herself."

"Some women are just selfish. She is not staying in that relationship for her children. She is staying because she still loves the man."

The hurt finger forgets about the pangs of childbirth, the difficulties of raising children, the complex dynamics of relationships and, generally, the reality of being human.

We need more compassion for each other. Because when we gather together as women, when we see ourselves in each other, when we listen with our hearts and hold each other through pain, we experience the sanctity of healing. A healing that can only be birthed by compassion and gentleness.

Every woman needs this nest. A space that is tucked away from the noise and demands of everyday living. A space where she can go to voice her worries and incubate her dreams. A space where we go to heal and experience true connection. To be reminded that we are valued and valuable. Where other women nod their heads in understanding, even without us having to explain.

We need the warmth and therapy that are transmitted through female communion. The counsel of those who have walked paths which may not be the same as ours, but which are in many ways similar. The wisdom of age. The untethered optimism of youth.

The nest is a space. But it is also a people. It is where we "give birth with other women".

THE DELICIOUS
GATHERING

They said: "Let's get together and bring something
to share.
Just us.
Women."

And so today we gathered.
Five women.
Generations apart
Bound in humanness
And womanness.

Raw conversations
Over masala spiced chicken
Bosnian tea
And orange cardamon cake.

From the table
To the fireplace
Delicious conversations

Absent telephones
No care for time.

Opening up hearts
Laying bare lives
Understanding
Communicating
No judgement
Absent resentment.

Talking through pain
Celebrating triumph
Tears …
Of joy
Of relief
Of hope
More cake
Dreams
Dares
Gratitude.

Stories
Of hilarious marriages
And shuttered marriages
Of devotion
And separation
Of children
And grandchildren
Of retirement
And retreat

Beginning life after experiencing death
Beginning life through new dreams
New love.

As the spirit travelled through us
A nest was created
A quilt of friendships
New and old
That would travel through generations and nations
From England to Pakistan
Bosnia to Ireland
Uganda to Canada.

As we stepped into the dark of the night
It didn't have to be said
That a new sisterhood had been birthed
Sparkling and strong
Just like a woman.

Relationship with Self

I HAD A HAPPY childhood.

Even though the early phases of our lives were punctuated with the brutality of the civil wars that ravaged Uganda in the 1970s and 1980s, my siblings and I carry mostly fond memories of our experiences growing up. We do recall times when we had to "take cover" under beds or classroom tables to escape the gunshots that were ringing in the air. We remember periods of food scarcity when people started hoarding rice, maize flour and beans. We recall the green army uniforms and thick boots that paraded the streets of Kampala. At some point, we had over ten relatives coming to seek refuge in our house. We remember these things. But mostly vaguely. What we recall more vividly is the white caravan that was parked in our large compound where we would play with our friends when they came to visit. We recall the grass food that we used to cook in old Blueband tins and the tummy aches that would follow. We reminisce about our family outings to Bimbo Icecream wearing our Sunday best and the thousands of times that we watched *The Sound of Music*, following which we would pretend to be a version of the Von Trapp family. Of course, I will never forget my first experience going to the cinema to watch *Coming to America*.

In 1986 we went into exile in Kenya. For our mother, this was a very difficult time. She had already lost some of her siblings to the war. Her once thriving businesses were no more. And now, she was forced to be separated from her best friend (her father), her fragile mother, her surviving siblings and her friends. She would be removed from the only place she had known as her home and transplanted in a foreign land. My stepfather, being Kenyan, was returning home.

To properly integrate into the social life and the business community in Kenya, our mother would need to learn Kiswahili and with time, some Luo. She moved from the familiarity of the streets of Wandegeya, a busy hub in Kampala where most of her family worked or lived, to the distant but neatly manicured lawns of a house in Tom Mboya, a middle class gated community in Kisumu. Her staple, *matooke* and *kinyebwa*, would be replaced with *ugali*, *sukuma wiki* and *nyama choma*. As if things were not bad enough, when she was in exile, she lost her father, her mother and some more of her siblings. She was not able to bury any of them. This, of course, broke her in more ways than one and she suffered numerous mental breakdowns. The only thing that kept her alive and gave her any appetite for living was us, her children.

Parents have a way of preserving their children's childhood by sheltering them from adversity. In contrast to the emotional turmoil that our mother was battling with internally, other than the slight inconvenience of changing area codes, ours was mostly a stable and happy childhood. Maybe that was because we were all relatively young and had the most important person in our lives – our mother – with us. I don't recall missing my school friends terribly or experiencing anguish over having to learn new languages. It all seemed very much like a long adventure. Before we knew it, we were running around the streets of Tom Mboya, climbing over neighbours' fences, speaking Kiswahili like the natives and walking the two kilometres from school to home with our new friends. Just like in Uganda, we continued to be immersed in play and enveloped by the security provided by our loving parents.

I loved to sing – a lot like my daughters do now. And even though my younger sisters confessed many years later that they were tortured by my tone-deaf voice, I thought of myself as quite a talented singer. I knew the lyrics to Tina Turner songs, Whitney Houston songs, Tracy Chapman songs and Bobby Brown songs. Oh yes, Vanilla Ice too. I even knew most "church songs", which our school friends had generously taught us after learning them at Sunday school. And when I ran out of other people's songs to sing, I would compose my own songs. My younger siblings had no option but to learn the songs. I had crowned myself the queen bee – and leader of the band. They had no option but to follow my orders.

Needless to say, I was a confident, vibrant and happy young girl. I climbed trees, entered myself into elocution contests at school and was the captain of the blue swimming team. I didn't spend much time thinking about beauty (other than those moments when I had to dress up as Tina Turner or Whitney Houston). I ran faster than many boys, played netball and volleyball and volunteered myself to be class representative for music class. I did not worry whether I was thin or fat. Whether I was light-skinned or dark-skinned. And I certainly didn't worry about the texture of my hair – apart from those times when the hot comb that was used to straighten our hair accidentally touched the skin of my ear.

And then, one day, I was informed that I was not beautiful. And I began to become aware of my lack of beauty. Over time, I convinced myself that in order to be loved, I had to use more of the things that I had (particularly my pear-shaped body and my academic intelligence) to compensate for the big hole that was created by my lack of beauty. Because I was not enough, I had to keep giving of myself without keeping for myself. Only then, I believed, would I be worthy of receiving love.

LITTLE GIRLS,
BIG WOMEN,
YOU ARE ENOUGH

S OMETIMES YOU DODGE THE bullets of war only to be scarred by seemingly immaterial events, such as the careless words uttered by a peer during a disagreement whose context you don't even remember. There are two main incidents that robbed me of my youthful bliss and sentenced me to a long and painful term of struggle with self. I was around nine years old when I had an argument with a girl in my class, who was known to be quarrelsome. I must have been winning the argument. And so, to shut me up, she shouted:

"That's why you are ugly! You have pimples all over your face!"

I shut up. And in many ways, I also shut down. I instantly became aware of what I looked like. And I started thinking that others must be looking at me as that ugly girl with pimples. Naturally, my confidence also plummeted.

The second incident was when I was in high school. I was around twelve or thirteen years old. This time round, it was not a quarrelsome girl. It was a male cousin who I not only looked up to but also considered as one of my favourite cousins. We were having a heated debate. I don't quite remember what we were arguing about. But again, I must have been winning. Because he felt the need to shut me up by saying:

"You will have to study really hard because you are not beautiful."

It was savage. And blurted out with an intention to silence. THAT – that was really painful and unsettling. Over time, I had been able to dismiss the comment of the girl in primary school because I kept reminding myself that she was just a quarrelsome girl. But how could I, as impressionable as I was, recover from such a blow by an older male that I looked up to? Had he been thinking this about me all these years? Is that what other people saw when they saw me?

Once again, I became insecure. I became resigned to the fact that I was doomed to be ugly. And I spent the rest of my teenage years and the bulk of my twenties and thirties trying to make up for my ugliness.

There were other incidents along the way. Like when I did not get the leading role in a high school play. Even though I had the right accent for the part and had qualified as one of the two final contestants, I did not have the looks. So, the part went to a pretty girl who had the looks (This, of course, is my interpretation of the decision-making process, which may or may not be true).

Then there was the pretty cousin who slept with a man that I was dating and later moved in with him. There were other incidents, each confirming what I already knew by now. I was not beautiful.

They say that every cloud has a silver lining. In my case, the lining was that because my cousin had assured me that I had to work hard, I took that as the gospel truth. Because I now knew that I could not rely on my physical beauty, I would have to rely on the beauty of my mind. Essentially, there were only two options: beautiful and loved or ugly and hardworking.

But like many young ladies, I still craved to be beautiful. Because to be beautiful was to be loved. To be beautiful was to be admired. To be beautiful was to be secure. It did not matter that my parents and siblings thought the world of me. I needed the acceptance and approval of others. And so, in secondary school, I found myself gravitating more towards the girls that were perceived to be beautiful (maybe, somehow, people would get confused and think that I too was beautiful?) And because beauty was often associated with how one relates to the opposite sex, I got into relationships that I shouldn't have because I felt like I was being done a favour. And when I was hurt and disappointed in those relationships, I knew without a doubt that if I had been beautiful, that would not have happened to me. That the person would not have cheated on me. The person would not have treated me like I did not matter. That person would not have talked to me like that.

One day, I watched an Oprah Winfrey show in which the smashingly beautiful actress, Halle Berry, was talking about how her husband, Eric Benet, cheated on her. I thought: *How is that even possible? How is it possible that anyone can cheat on this woman who has such a gorgeous face and a body to die for? How?* After that, I started noticing how women that I knew personally and considered to be beautiful were being cheated on by their men. Some of them were in abusive relationships. Others did not even have men (because obviously if you are that beautiful, you should have a man, right?) When I spoke with them, I found out that they too had been "unbeautified". They had been told that they were nagging. They had been told that they were fat. They had been told that they had put stories in their heads about their men's transgressions. They had been told that they were too loud or uncultured.

The thing about feeling like you are not enough is that you feel a need to overcompensate. Constantly. You blame yourself for other peoples' inadequacies and, many times, their insecurities. You allow yourself to be abused – physically and emotionally.

It took me decades to embrace myself. To define myself for myself. It took drinking from the fountains of women who had fully embraced their womanhood. The wise counselling of women that I had never met – mothers like Maya Angelou, whose poetry and stories made me spring to life. Artists like India Arie, who, in her song "Video", challenged me to learn "to love myself unconditionally, because I am a queen". It took meeting a man (now my husband) who seemed totally oblivious of the many things that caused my insecurity. It took strangers telling me that I brightened their days with my beautiful smile. And unfortunately, it also took me seeing that the women that I thought of as beautiful were also experiencing emotional hardships.

It also helped when I constantly heard from my friends that I was a great friend and a confidante. It was a boost to my confidence when my mentors told me that I had a brilliant idea and said that they recommended me highly. It helped when my sisters said that they could rely on me and when my mother said that she needed me to communicate something to someone because I had a way of speaking with people.

But mostly, it took me getting into the tough business of falling in love with my whole self. Knowing that I had to save me. I had to love me. No one was going to do that part of the work for me, however much they loved me.

In her powerful book, *The Choice*, psychologist and holocaust survivor, Edith Eger, ends with a compelling message:

> And here you are. Here you are! In the sacred present. I can't heal you – or anyone – but I can celebrate your choice to dismantle the prison in your mind, brick by brick. You can't change what happened, you can't change what you did or what was done to you. But you can choose how you live *now*.

> My precious, you can choose to be free.

Almost three decades ago, a young girl called me ugly. A few years later, my male cousin told me that I was not beautiful. These were not nice things to say. Words can make or break. And often, it doesn't matter how young or how old we are. There is a little girl or a little boy inside each and every one of us that simply hungers for acceptance, in whatever form it takes. But the beauty of life is that we also get to choose. We get to choose whether we let words or people break us or make us. For decades, I chose to let those words define me and reduce me. I chose those words over the loving words of my family. I chose those words over the admiration of my friends. I chose those words over the words of a man who told me that I was beautiful. And I chose those words over the unconditional love expressed by two precious beings, my daughters.

Today, I choose something else. I choose to love myself.

Little girls. Big women. You are enough. But only you decide your "enough-ness". Only you define your worth. Only you determine how you want others to treat you. The things that make you happy. The shade(s) of beauty that define you.

You get to choose.

I hope you choose you.

Do You Love Yourself
Enough?

R AE WAS ONE OF my first friends when I joined Nabisunsa Girls School. Even though she was one year
ahead of me, we soon became best friends. It was the raw,
sweet and intense kind of teenage friendship. The kind
where you are prepared to split your last grain of *meketu*
(a hard corn delicacy that was much loved in boarding
school, particularly in the later months of the term when
most had run out of snacks and pocket money). Rae was
also a brilliant writer. So precious was our friendship that
when she wrote novels in the Picfare exercise books that
we used for our school work, she put both our names as
authors on the blue cover.

Even though this kind of selfless friendship came naturally to Rae, I struggled with it. I tried to reciprocate
it. But I also fought it. One minute I was her best friend
and the next minute I was doing something to deliberately hurt her feelings. When Rae was nominated as the
Chairlady of the "social" (the equivalent of prom Queen)

for her year group, most of the girls at school were happy for her because she was dearly loved. As her best friend, I should have been the happiest. Instead, I was jealous. Or maybe, I was just afraid. I was jealous of her popularity, which meant that she would probably get new friends; better friends than me. That made me afraid. I tried to make her feel guilty for being chosen. I belittled the social as a petty and meaningless event. And at some point, I just stopped talking to her (something that I had done on several occasions before as a way of punishing her). For over two years, Rae had patiently massaged my delicate ego, doing everything to reassure me that I was indeed her best friend. But it can be exhausting having to bury one's own happiness for a person who is constantly chasing away happiness. My hostile behaviour leading to the social was Rae's turning point. She had had enough. She finally entertained the idea of widening her pool of close friendships. And eventually, she found a clan of girls who treasured the worth of her friendship and did not punish her for her ability to love. Friends who did not need to crush her spirit in an attempt to repair their own.

When you do not feel worthy, you do not think that you are worthy of good things. And so, when good things present themselves in your life, you fight them and try as much as possible to chase them away. I had not learnt my lesson from the breaking of my close friendship with Rae. History would of course repeat itself. My struggle with self-love showed up again when I met the man who is now my husband. When he would tell me that I was beautiful, I would quickly respond, "Thanks. But my breasts are too small." Or "Thanks. But I have pimples on my face." "I have put on weight." My insecurities also meant that I was obsessed with finding out about his past relationship. *Was his ex-girlfriend pretty? Did his mother like her? Did his mother like her because she was pretty (prettier than me)? Did he have any pictures of hers that I could look at? Were they still friends? Did he really mean it when he said that I was beautiful? Did he wish I was as beautiful as his ex-girlfriend (the one I had never seen)?* I was in need of constant reassurance. I needed proof that I was both loved and lovable. At first, he would humour me. "No, your breasts are not too small. They are actually a really good size." "You look great! I don't see the weight you are talking about." But he soon got exhausted. He probably realized that he could not love me enough for both of us. And so he stopped reassuring me. And when he stopped, I started to panic and sulk. *Did he not love me anymore? Had he found someone who was more lovable? Was he lying when he said I was beautiful?* At some point, he decided that he had had enough. He was incapable of rescuing me. So he let go.

One of Rae's favourite quotes when we were in secondary school was: "If you love something, let it go. If it comes back to you, it truly is yours. If it doesn't, it never was yours." In my very twisted way, I was both incapable of letting go and of holding on. What I majored in was testing. Experimenting. Testing those who loved me by trying to figure out whether they loved me enough. Pushing them away in the hope that they would stick. And other times, holding on so tight that they felt suffocated.

This was not limited to my interactions with Rae and my husband. Over the years, I did this with other friends and family too. When I was disturbed by a thought that I had difficulty processing or an unpleasant feeling, instead of being curious about why I was feeling the way I was feeling, I would remove the burden of having to think about it from myself and deposit it heavily on another person. Instead of asking someone a question about my perception of something that they had said or done, I would blurt out things that I had not carefully thought through in an attempt to dislodge the discomfort in my chest. I would hit back at the other person snappily in an attempt to protect myself. I would rush to conclusions instead of seeking explanations. My relief was normally short-lived. But the burden that I had deposited on the other person was not.

When my husband (then boyfriend) shut me out, I was forced to confront my demons. I had to unpack why it was that I was hurting the people who loved me. *What was it that I was running away from? Why did I feel the need to hit hard and hit low? What was I afraid of? Whose responsibility was it to love me?*

These have been uncomfortable emotions to unpick. And while I have made significant progress over the years, I am still on the wobbly journey of learning to let go of the fear of abandonment.

A person who does not love themselves is extremely difficult, if not impossible, to love. They constantly get in the way of love. I have finally come to the realization that, however much someone loves me, if I do not love myself, that love from another will never be enough. I also realize that at some point, even the people who love you dearly get exhausted and need to protect themselves from all the venom that is spewing out of you.

I still have moments. Moments when I have a disagreement with my husband and think: is this fight going to lead to the breakdown of our marriage? Moments when I find out that a friend's husband has been unfaithful and I wonder: is it my turn next? Moments when a couple that I admire announces the shocking news that they are breaking up and I worry: is this where we are eventually heading to? During these moments, I crawl back into my deep-seated fear of abandonment. And I start to armour up. I tell myself that if I learn to guard my emotions and not become too vulnerable, too emotionally available, I will not get hurt if my marriage fails. If I succeed at my career, it will not matter so much if my marriage fails. Because at least I will still have something going on for me. If I lose weight and fix the blemishes on my face, maybe he will not leave me. And if he does leave me, I will not experience as much shame because at least I will look great. At least I will still be desirable. And then there is the mother of all armours: I can do it without him. I don't need a man in my life.

Except, this is not really living. I cannot live fully today when I am in fear of what might happen tomorrow or a few hours from now. I cannot tap into the joy that love brings when I wear armour intended to protect me from the pain associated with loving. I cannot experience what it truly means to be human when I am obsessed with controlling the uncontrollable. And so, I have to constantly remind myself that I am not in control. Nothing in life is guaranteed. I have no control over whether my husband will love me or leave me. I have no control over what kind of grown-ups my children will choose to be. I have no control over whether I will live until I am 93 or whether I will die tomorrow. But I do have control over the things that I choose to magnify. I have control over the thoughts that occupy my mind. And one of the kindest things that I can do for myself is to choose peace of mind. I am not always successful. But I will die trying.

Remember... "You're Not in It"

WHEN I HAD JUST started my last job, I was messing up big time. I didn't seem to be getting anything right. It took me ages to do things that others seemed to do in minutes. I sent out emails that I wanted to recall immediately. I felt dumb about the contributions that I made in team meetings. I wrote papers that were returned with red marks all over. I felt like I was failing miserably. And I beat myself up again and again. Every time I saw my colleagues whispering or laughing about something, I imagined that they must be talking about me or laughing at me. They must be talking about the fact that I didn't know what I was doing. They must be wondering how I got the job. They must be thinking that I am a complete idiot. Obviously, my thoughts did not help things. The more I obsessed about what they must be thinking, the less I was able to focus and perform to my fullest potential. This invariably led to more messing up.

Then one day, I watched a video of one of Oprah Winfrey's life classes where she was talking about how, earlier in her career, she called Maya Angelou, crying about something that had been written about her (Oprah) in the newspapers, which was not true. Maya told her, "You are not in it." Oprah continued: "But Maya, they said this and this and this and it's not true and ..." Maya repeated: "Oprah, you are not in it. People will try to peck you to death like a duck. But remember, you're not in it."

What Maya meant was that we cannot control what people think about us. We cannot control what people say about us. We cannot control what people feel about us. The only control we have is over ourselves. Just because someone chooses to talk about you does not mean you have to invest your own emotions in what they are saying or thinking. "You're not in it."

That was a life-changing moment for me.

I realized that the problem was not with my colleagues. The problem was that I was spending too much time obsessing over what others thought of me. It was not the first time I was experiencing these kinds of emotions. Indeed, they were not restricted to my professional life. For far too long, I had allowed people to peck at me by caring so much about what they thought of me. By wanting people to like me. To approve of me. To keep cheering me on.

I have often been a permission seeker. A people pleaser. A goody-two-shoes. And so it took me a while to breathe in Maya's words and weave them into my everyday being. But once I did, I felt liberated and empowered. Not in a braggadocio kind of way, but in a way that ushered in peace of mind.

Now, when I see people whispering while looking suspiciously in my direction, I remind myself that I am not in it. When I read a post on Facebook, which seems targeted at me, I remind myself that I am not in it. When someone who is supposed to be my friend chooses to talk behind my back instead of coming to me, I remind myself that I am not in it. When a colleague says hello in a detached manner or when they seem to be avoiding me, I remind myself that I am not in it.

But I also remind myself that people's lives do not revolve around me. It is quite possible that they have their internal jokes. They might be whispering or laughing at something that has nothing at all to do with me. When someone is friendly one minute and distant the next, I tell myself that it is not about me. Maybe they are having problems at home. Maybe they are feeling ill. Maybe they just found out some bad news about a loved one. Maybe they just hate their job. Maybe they just lost their job. Maybe they are drowning in debt. Or maybe they just don't want to say hello.

Whatever it is, I am not in it. If they haven't confided in me, unfortunately, I cannot be of service (assuming they even need my service). And if it is the case that they just don't like me, well, that is their business, not mine. Either way, I am not in it.

Many times in life we allow people to peck at us. We give people the power to dictate our moods. We wait for people to give us permission on when to be happy.

JALIA KANGAVE

We let the words of others sting us, even when we know that what they are saying is not true. Other times, we tell ourselves stories about what people must be thinking of us. We convince ourselves that people wake up thinking about how to make our lives miserable and go to bed celebrating the misery they have created in our lives. We give people significant shares in our precious lives. In the process, we hand our happiness over to them. We let them feed their misery by sucking on us. We allow them to rob us of our happiness. To disable our creativity. To distort our reality.

The result?

We shrink. We begin to second-guess ourselves. We retreat from the things that send music to our hearts. We get "in it" with them.

That is not living. That is not being alive. That is handing the remote control of your life to someone else.

Only you have control over your feelings. You do not have control over what someone says about you or feels about you. But you have control over how you react to it.

Don't let the actions or words of others reduce you.

Remember… "You're not in it."

Guarding Your
Mental Space

THERE ARE GOING TO be times in your life when, for whatever reason, people are going to try and drag you through the mud with them. Suck you into their misery. It is not always evident that they are doing this. And it takes different forms. It may be in the tone that a colleague chooses to use in an email. Or in the passive aggressive behaviour of a friend or a sibling who insists that there is nothing wrong or that they don't know what you are talking about, when the vibes that they send you speak otherwise. Sometimes it is in the silence of a spouse who has wronged you but who expects you to apologize. Or in the actions of a boss who makes you second-guess yourself. Other times it is in the lamenting of a parent who makes you question whether you will ever measure up to their expectations.

In each of these instances, you may feel tempted to explain yourself. To try and demonstrate that you are actually a good person. To show that you have been misunderstood. Sometimes, you may even be tempted to play victim.

Check yourself. And if you find a clean bill of health, remind yourself that you are not the problem. They are. You have no control over their actions. The only control you have is over you.

Guard your mental space. It is sacred.

P.S: This is a note to myself.

Dear Sister, Love Yourself Enough

D EAR SISTER,
Love yourself enough to know when you deserve better.

Love yourself enough to ask for the things that you desire in a relationship.

Love yourself enough to stop beating yourself up over the mistakes that you made in the past. In fact, love yourself enough to laugh at your mistakes. To remind yourself, as Maya Angelou is often quoted as saying, "When you know better, you do better."

Love yourself enough not to feel the need to put another woman down. To see in that woman a reflection of yourself.

Love yourself enough to laugh at those voices in your head which keep tricking you into thinking that you are less than. Telling you that "You are not beautiful enough." "You are not intelligent enough." "You cannot succeed at that business." "You cannot survive without that relationship." "You are too old to start afresh."

Love yourself enough not to partake in any kind of drama that serves the purpose of nibbling at the peace of your mind. Tell yourself: "Nope. Not my cup of tea. I am not in it."

Love yourself enough to know that it is okay to take care of yourself. To put your feet up even before you tire. To spend the day revelling in a book that breathes life into your soul. To meet up with girlfriends who tickle your heart. Or simply, to spend some time basking in your own awesomeness.

Love yourself enough to find no guilt in saying "no". To not drown in endless demands on your time. Take care of you.

Love yourself enough to enjoy the fine things in life. You have worked hard for them. You deserve the treat.

Love yourself enough to have an income that will buy you some form of financial and/or mental freedom.

Just. Love. Yourself. Enough.

2020 Part 1: What Do You Say to Yourself Every Morning?

20 was a pretty tough year. The coronavirus pandemic brought many of us to our knees. In some ways, 2021 seems like an extension of 2020. Some of us are having a difficult time home schooling our children. Others are stuck at home, day in day out, without any clear indications of an expiry date to lockdowns. Others have closed businesses in which they invested life savings and do not know how they will feed their families for the coming months, let alone the coming days. Some have lost their loved ones. Others have lost jobs.

Many of these experiences are, of course, not new. But the pandemic has created new layers of complexity.

Some of us are sad. Some of us are frustrated. Some of us are anxious. Some of us are depressed. Some of us are angry. Many are feeling hopeless. Buried under all these feelings is one constant: fear.

We are afraid.

And when we are afraid, we tend to lash out. We yell at our children. We say things to our loved ones that we wish we could take back. We consume shameful quantities and qualities of food. And we try to distract ourselves by devouring equally shameful quantities of television and social media.

The result?

We start feeling terrible about ourselves. We feel terrible that we did not follow through with the goals that we set. We feel terrible that we yelled at our little ones or said mean things to our loved ones or colleagues. We feel terrible that we are not measuring up to the person that we want to be.

And when we feel terrible about ourselves, we wake up the next morning and beat ourselves up.

I don't know about you, but as for me, when I beat myself up, I tend to feel worse. I think: *What's the point anyway? I am already damaged goods. I am irreparable.* And because I feel worse, I do worse. I eat more chocolate and crisps. I yell more. I spend more aimless time on social media. And then the next day, I feel even worse. So, clearly, beating myself up is not making me feel any better about myself.

Instead of beating myself up, I am learning to be more compassionate with myself. Every morning, I take an audit of my actions of the day before. But instead of starting with what I did poorly, I start with what I did well. I went for a walk yesterday. Tick. I sent out that email that I have been meaning to send out. Tick. On one occasion, I kept quiet instead of saying hurtful words to a loved one. Tick. I cuddled my daughter when she cried instead of ostracizing her. Tick. I drank a litre of water. Tick. I called a friend to find out how she was holding up, given her recent loss. Tick.

I go through all the things that I did well, however immaterial they may seem. I pat myself on the back for a job well done. And then I ask myself what I could have done better. How could I have been more kind? How could I have been more patient? How could I have been more understanding? How could I have been more productive?

Many things or people in life are going to beat us up. But we don't have to join them. We need to learn to be gentle with ourselves. We need to learn to be more forgiving of ourselves. More patient with ourselves. It does not mean that we are making excuses for our poor behaviour. It just means that we are acknowledging that we are human. We make mistakes. We fall and falter. But we can do better. We will do better.

And maybe, when we learn to be more compassionate with ourselves, we are more likely to extend that compassion to others.

The Baggage
We Carry Around

In the song "Bag Lady", the phenomenal Erykah Badu sings about the baggage that women carry around, warning us that all this baggage is going to get in our way. "Bag lady you gone hurt your back, dragging all them bags like that." Let go, she says. "You got too much stuff."

Women have been duped into believing that martyrdom is the highest expression of ourselves. That we need to go through some form of suffering to prove our worth as women. That perfection should be our ultimate goal. That our worth is determined by how long we stay in marriage, how clean we keep our homes, how well our children present in public, our ability to cook meals from scratch every day of the week and how intact we can keep our bodies after giving birth. We have been made to believe that when our marriages fail, it is because we are lacking in some respect. When our children misbehave, it is because we are not good mothers. When our bodies give way, it is because we have been careless.

We carry the world's baggage on our shoulders. And it is eating us up. We have set ourselves or let society set for us expectations that are not achievable. We are running after Neverland.

The Baganda have a common expression: *guma*. The literal translation is "be strong". It is commonly uttered to women who are experiencing difficulties in their relationships. Women are expected to be strong when their men cheat on them. Women are expected to be strong when their backs break from too much work. Women are expected to be strong when they give birth. Women are expected to be strong, even when they lose a loved one. It is considered a form of praise when a woman is referred to as strong. But what is the cost of this strength?

What Is the Cost of
Our Strength
as Women?

W<small>HEN</small> I <small>HAD JUST</small> got married, and in fact for the first five or so years into marriage, I wanted to prove that I was superwoman. I wanted to show my husband (and the outside world) that in addition to my ability to hold intelligent conversations and contribute to our household income, I could also make delicious meals from scratch, keep the house as clean as a hospital operating room, and, at the end of the day, still be in a position to perform acrobatics in bed. I was bent on proving to myself and to others that I could be a combination of super mum, super wife and super employee. But mostly, I was concerned with demonstrating my perfection to my husband: *Do you see me? Do you see how hardworking I am? Do you see how nice I am? Do you see how much money I am able to save us? Does your family know all these things that I bring to the table? Do you know the trophy of a woman that you won?* When my husband would reminisce about some of the things that his mother used to do when they were growing up, I would make a mental note to do them bigger and better. I was, after all, a keeper.

At two and three years old, our daughters had their first play date with their friend from nursery. She came with her dad. They had been playing for a whole ten minutes when one of them accidentally spilled their juice. I quickly ran to the kitchen to get a mop to clean after them. Throughout the two-hour play date, I dutifully hovered over the three toddlers, with the zeal of a newly appointed class monitor, eager to write down the names of noise makers. With a dustpan and little broom on standby, I swept after each crumb that fell. Rice cake crumbs. Sweep. Mini cheddars. Sweep. Juice. Mop. Grapes. Sweep. Pom-Bears. Sweep. It didn't bother me that their friend's dad fidgeted uncomfortably at the edge of his seat, probably counting down to the end of the playdate.

Even though I had a two and a three-year old, my house was normally sparkly clean. The cream carpet carried no evidence of having toddlers in the house. The girls' toys were neatly tucked away in a corner in the living room – each toy put away as soon as my surveillance had determined that they were not playing with it at that particular time. It was more important to have a clean house than messy happy children. A clean house meant that I was a good woman: another symbol of my strength.

There's a level of virtuousness attached to the strength of a woman. A strong woman takes it all in her stride. A

JALIA KANGAVE

strong woman does not complain. A strong woman can do it all. A strong woman is a good woman. A strong woman is to be admired. An essential ingredient of being strong is, of course, demonstrating that you are not weak. In other words, you do not go for the easier options when you can make your life a little more complicated. Your worth becomes tied to the things that you do. *I am more worthy when I make fresh breakfast daily instead of giving the kids boxed cereal. I am more worthy when I hand wash the dishes instead of using the dishwasher. I am more worthy when I make fresh meals every single day, despite complaining of being chronically exhausted. The more I choose the tougher route over the gentler route, the more valuable I will be. My husband will love me more. My children will confirm that their mother loves them dearly.*

We have been socialised to think that the harder we work, the more lovable we will be. Meanwhile, our men do not take part in these pageants. As we kill ourselves to prove our worth, they – for the most part – are just concerned with being. *Just being.* As we shrink down our circle of relations to our nuclear family unit, they continue to hang out with the boys. Even when they give the best at work, at home, many of them get away with doing the absolute minimum. And praise be to them, every now and then, they "babysit" their own children. In the end, they do not put themselves under the same kind of pressure that we put ourselves under (or that society puts on us).

The consequence? Two things – burnout and bitterness.

We suffer from chronic exhaustion, hoping that someone (clue: the male in the house) will at some point say: "You have done so much darling. Please take a break."

Alas. That message rarely comes. And so, we become resentful. We become resentful because we feel like we are not being appreciated. We become resentful because no one seems to notice how hard we work. We become worn out – physically and emotionally.

I have often heard women and men talk proudly about their mothers who never complained about anything. They just silently and diligently went about their work. Even when the work was killing them. They did not want to burden their children by letting them know what they were going through. In some cases, they were too scared to tell their husbands. Sometimes they didn't even share their burdens with their female friends. They did not want to be thought of as weak.

When I hear people praise our mothers and grandmothers, I want to ask them: Have you ever really asked our mothers and grandmothers how they felt about all this work? Whether they could have done with more help? Whether they had a choice? Have you cared to find out what these unrealistic expectations did to their mental health? Can you entertain the possibility that our mothers would have appreciated a day off?

Anyway, about two years ago, I decided that I was incapable of being a strong woman. In fact, I did not desire to be one. I decided that I wanted my children to know that Maama is not a supershero. Maama gets tired. Maama needs to take a break every now and then.

Maama needs to recharge her batteries (afternoon nap anyone?).

Every now and then, I will hear my daughters saying: "We need to tidy up because Maama's back will hurt if she does too much work." Or "Maama, do you need a massage?" Also, really, teamwork is dreamwork (obviously not my words but I couldn't agree more). I needed my children to know from a very young age that each and every one of us is human. Even Maama. Maama needs to put her feet up. She needs to take a break. And we need to collectively participate in keeping this small community of ours in order.

As for my husband, I am no longer in the business of equating hard work with being a good wife. I am quite happy being an imperfect wife. I have no need to measure up to his mother or his sister or so and so's wife. I am pretty content not being a strong woman (whatever that means).

Do You Stop to Smell
the Coffee?

Many years ago, when I was visiting relatives and friends in the United States, a woman in the Ugandan community in Boston who had no known illness, collapsed and died. I was told that the woman had been a workaholic. She worked almost every minute of her life – sometimes 24 hours straight, moving from one job to another. She rarely attended social gatherings. She was working hard to send money back home to Uganda in the hope that after a few years she would return home and enjoy a slower life. She didn't get to enjoy her hard-earned money. She died in her forties.

It was difficult for me at the time – as a young, privileged, university student – to fathom how someone could work themselves to death. But I can now see how easily this can happen. Even when the work doesn't drive you to death, I can see how the constant movement, the constant pressure to do and deliver, can give someone a nervous breakdown. At the very least, I can see how it takes away the moments of pleasure that we are all presumably working towards.

Work never ends – whether it be in the office or in the home. There will always be something pending. The email to respond to. The laundry to do. The assignment to hand in. The dishes to wash. The meeting to attend. The dentist's appointment to schedule. The conference to attend. The meals to prepare. The proposal to write. The homework to check. The CV to update. The nails to clip. The account to close. Many of us are living on conveyor belts. Only you can press the stop button. And you should. Frequently.

It is important that we get into the habit of taking care of ourselves. Of stopping to smell the coffee. As a full-time working mum (N.B.: most mothers are full-time working mums), I am quickly learning that I am the only one who can give myself a break. I am the only one who can say: "I know that I could complete that assignment if I killed myself (because I want to impress my boss), but I really don't want to die. I don't want my tank to be running on empty. I need to reserve some fuel for tomorrow." I am learning to say no. Or, not now.

I know that I can keep the house squeaky clean, make perfect meals from scratch (accompanied with different flavours of home-made smoothies) and iron all the clothes before I put them away in the wardrobes. All in good time for the bedtime story. But I would be doing that at the expense of my health or sanity, if not both. I don't want to die. And so, I have learnt to say, "not today" and to say to myself instead, "That hair looks a little raggedy but look at that happy child who is well fed!"

I have also learnt to ask for help. I used to think of "help" and "ask" as dirty words. I also thought it should be quite obvious that if people are living in the same house and there's work to be done, as long as there are no robots in that house, that work would have to be shared by the human occupants. It turns out that even a genius of a man is not always attuned to the stuff that needs to be done. And so, after almost dislocating my face because I was pulling it in all sorts of directions waiting for my husband to figure out that he needed to do more, I dared to use the dirty words: *I need your help*. I understand that some women find it ridiculous to use the word "help" because this implies that it is the woman's responsibility to do all the work around the house and that the man gets to choose when to participate. I used to find it ridiculous to ask for help too. But I have been much happier since I started doing so. I obviously look forward to a time when women will not have to make negotiations in this way. But I leave that battle to someone else.

Back to my point about coffee – I now stop more to smell the coffee. I relax. I breathe. I put my bags down. I read a book that I love. I listen to music that tickles my soul. I sit on the sofa doing nothing other than watching two little people squabbling and then making up. Sometimes, we are in the centre of a mess. But I know that tomorrow is also a day. I am reminded of the wise words of my Nigerian friend Chilenye: "It is not a do or die affair."

Every time I am able to do this, every time I let go and remind myself that I am not here to solve all of the world's problems, that I am not Miss Perfect, a friendly voice whispers that I need to do nothing more often. It is good for me. It is good for my family. In fact, it is good for society.

I Want to Stop

I want to stop
Looking at the pop-up window
Of my laptop
Waiting for the beep
On my phone.

I need to stop
Breathe in the pleasure of nothingness
And exhale the pressure of anxiety.

I want to stop
Pay tribute to the depth of conversations
Hear the words
Coming out of the mouths
Of babes
Taste the tingle of ginger lemon tea.

I want to let go
Of the baggage of expectations
Say no to endless demands

On my time
On my mind
On my body.

I need to stop
Listen to the murmurs of my heart
Pay attention
To the sting of my pain.

I want to stop
And travel through the pages of books
Immerse myself
In the wonders of nature.
I just want to stop.

But I have been waiting for permission
Approval
Perhaps even
Some accommodation
From my children
My husband
My employer
And sadly
Yes, even strangers.
It's not coming
It never will.

So am just going to stop.
For me.

THE BUG OF SMALLNESS

Female chickens normally do not crow. At least popular mythology claims that they cannot. Hence, in many African cultures a crowing hen is considered an omen of bad tidings that must be expiated through the immediate slaughter of the offending bird.

Sylvia Tamale, **When Hens Begin to Crow**

INCIDENTALLY, WHILE WOMEN ARE normally expected to be strong, there is also an expectation on us to act weak – or, more accurately, to act small. I can think of a few images. Damsel in distress. Knight in shining armour. Be seen but not heard.

Women are socialised to act small in order to accommodate fragile egos. *Don't be too loud – it is not ladylike. Don't be too confident – it is bossy. Don't speak about your accomplishments – it is showing off (and God doesn't like proud people). Don't announce your victories – it will make some people feel bad. Don't show anger – you will not be liked. Don't express your happiness. There are people who are having a hard time.*

Having become so accustomed to smallness, I normally have a quick rebuttal for any attempt intended at elevating me.

"Your hair looks gorgeous!" Me: "Thanks, it can get quite unruly sometimes."

"You are looking absolutely smashing in that dress!" Me: "Thanks. It's a cheap dress. It cost only £4.50. I bought it from Primark."

"You are looking great!" Me: "Oh thanks. I put on a few kilos though. This dress has a way of hiding them."

"That was a great presentation!" Me: "Oh thanks. But I messed up that part of it..."

I was socialised to think that if I acted like I was less capable, if I acted like I needed reassurance from a man, I could keep the man. He would not be threatened by me. He would find me more desirable. And so, when I had just got married, I played the role of the damsel in distress. Even when I knew the answer to something or had already made up my mind about something, I would still ask my husband a question about it to remind him that I needed him. I did not want to appear strong and capable of making independent decisions. I wanted him to know that I depended on him. That I could not do without him. That he really was my saviour.

I had heard – too frequently – both men and women say that men did not like women who were more educated than them. Indeed, some women said – and still say – that they did not date men who had a lower level of education than them. When I was going to pursue my Master's degree, one of my male cousins kindly warned me: "You already have a law degree. Now you are going to do a Master's?! You are going to have a difficult time finding a man!" Now, here I was, having the huge burden of a PhD and a well-paying job. The only way that I could keep my man was by ensuring that I acted smaller than I was. *Ask questions frequently. Slant your head a bit to show puzzlement and despair at the time of asking the question. If possible, lean on his shoulder just to show how much support you need. Repeat this exercise for the next question.*

This is a whole lot of baggage to carry around. And it really is an insult to intelligent men. There is, of course, nothing wrong with consulting in a relationship. And I have found that since I started consulting my husband meaningfully, I see the value addition that he makes to my individual and our collective goals. There is, however, a risk to "fake asking". When we get accustomed to acting small (or asking small), we eventually start to think we are actually small. We are no longer able to tap into our strengths. And I realized that that is where I was headed. So I stopped. And, surprise, surprise, my husband can handle an intelligent woman.

Even though I have made significant progress in this regard, I still fall into the trap of smallness every now and then. Smallness was not simply restricted to my relationship with my husband. It appeared frequently in the manner in which I related with other people too. And I have noticed that if I am not mindful enough, I can easily slip into smallness, particularly when I am not brave enough to take a stand. I experienced this last year.

A mum-friend at my daughters' school asked me what my view was about the government's announcement that schools in the UK would reopen in June 2020, after the first coronavirus-related countrywide lockdown. I told her that I thought it was still too early and that I did not feel it was safe yet for the children to go back. She told me that she felt the same way. She added that she had asked me because she valued my opinion (which, of course, made me feel valuable). A few days after our chat, there was a virtual school meeting, where the school administration informed us of the strategies that they were taking to ensure that our children would be kept as safe as possible if schools were to reopen. That meeting was reassuring. I also had a conversation with my sister Nadia, who is a nurse, which further convinced me that sending our daughters back to school was not a bad idea. I contacted my mum-friend and asked her what she thought after the school meeting. She replied that she was still going to keep her child at home since she still felt that it was too early to go back. And at least, she added, she and her husband still had jobs, which meant that they didn't have the same financial pressures that some families had.

I started to panic. *What will she think of me when she finds out that I have changed my mind? Will she remain friends with me? Will she still value my opinions? Will she tell the other mums and her husband how I flip-flopped? Will she start avoiding me? What should I do? What should I tell her? Help! Help!*

In my text message reply to her, I said: "We are going to mull over it today and weigh the options, taking personal circumstances into account. It is such a difficult time for everyone!" For emphasis, I added a crying emoji.

The truth was that, after hearing what the school had said and consulting with my sister, my husband and I had already discussed and decided that if there was a chance of sending our daughters back to school, we would do so. But I was not brave enough to tell her that I had changed my mind. I used the reference to "personal circumstances" as my armour. It was meant to shield me from any judgements that may have come from her. "Personal circumstances" may have made her wonder whether we were struggling to feed our children. "Personal circumstances" may have caused her to sympathize with my change of mind. "Personal circumstances" also meant that it would be uncomfortable for her to ask more questions. She would just have to empathize with me, believing that this must have been a really tough decision on our part.

While, like many families, it was true that the coronavirus and associated lockdown had affected our income, we were in a fortunate enough position to still have some work coming our way and so financial hardship was not the reason why we were opting to send our daughters back to school. The main reason was that we had changed our minds after acquiring new information. But because I had become so accustomed to making myself small to avoid being attacked, because I had become so accustomed to acting weak when I did not have the courage to speak my truth, smallness had become my default when things got tough.

The moment I sent that text message, I cringed. I recognized the baggage that I still carried around after all these years – the baggage of desperately seeking for acceptance and approval. And the bags came tumbling down.

The bag of not owning my truth.

The people pleaser.

The peace maker.

The goody-two-shoes.

The smiley one – even when her anger is justified.

The one who, when faced with opposing views, chooses silence because it was the safest.

The one who wants desperately to be liked.

I felt terrible.

What I also realized after that day is that it is okay to change my mind. This seems obvious, doesn't it? When I get to the counter at the supermarket and find that I should have picked vanilla ice cream instead of chocolate ice cream, I go back and pick vanilla ice cream. And yet, it was much harder for me to say that I had changed my mind when it came to the things that I had committed to, or even half committed to. I was afraid to change my mind because I feared that I would be letting the other person down. I was afraid to say that I changed my mind because I feared that the other person would think of me as unreliable (which meant that they might also stop liking me or stop trusting me or stop valuing my opinion or stop inviting me to parties).

That is a whole lot of baggage to carry around!

Here is the thing that I am learning about courage. Maya Angelou often said, "One isn't born with courage.

One develops it. And you develop it by doing small, courageous things."

So, here's to the journey of courage. Of not needing to manipulate situations or people in order to go after the things that serve me. Of not abusing vulnerability, because there will be times when I am genuinely vulnerable. Of being brave. One small act after another.

"I Am a Human Being. Nothing Human Is Alien to Me."
~ Terence

A FEW YEARS AGO, I asked my husband a question. As soon as the question was released from my mouth, I wanted to chase after it and grab it back before it reached his ears. But the words had been uttered. It was not really a question. It was an accusation. The words were sharp and tactless. They were meant to bite. And they did. His face received them with a mixture of confusion and disappointment. Still, he answered the question. And then he withdrew. In the weeks that followed, a heavy gloom hung around the house. Not even the naughty shrieks of our daughters could pierce through it. I said sorry. Several times. Each time, my husband responded that I shouldn't be sorry. As far as he was concerned, I had said what had probably been on my mind for a long time.

By this time, I had done a lot of personal growth work. And I somehow thought that I had figured life out. As they say, I thought I had arrived. Because I had written Facebook posts which had led a number of people into my inbox seeking advice about different things, including their relationships, I thought that I had become an expert on emotions. Because I spoke confidently and responded intelligently to personal and professional questions, I thought I had become an expert on living. I seemed to have mastered the art of communication. I was the calm one. The wise one. I had my act together. And as far as my relationships were concerned, I didn't do tantrums and drama anymore. Given how much I had grown over the years, I – consciously and subconsciously – perceived myself as being better than others. I was not the kind of woman who asked the kind of question that I had asked my husband – at least not that tactlessly. I was not the kind of woman who was unable to control my emotions. I was above all that. I was much better than that.

Imagine then the torture associated with having to come to terms with the realization that I was, after all, human. That I am one of those women who don't process what they are about to say before they talk. A woman who is not in control of her emotions.

In the weeks that followed, I beat myself up over and over again. I replayed my words and cringed each time they rang in my ears. I scolded myself again and again. I didn't need anyone to put me down. I was doing a pretty good job of it.

I had somehow managed to convince myself that I had become superhuman. Somewhere along the way on my growth journey, I had forgotten that "I am a human being. Nothing human is alien to me." Just because my emotional mileage had registered positive growth did not mean that I had arrived. Just because I managed to control my emotions every now and then did not mean that I was better than those who lost control every now and then. Just because I could remain calm most of the time did not mean that I was not prone to emotional meltdowns.

Maya Angelou often said, "I am trying to be a Christian." By this, she meant that she was trying to be the best that she could, recognizing that as long as she was alive, she was bound to fall and falter every now and then.

There is no painless way of having to come down off a pedestal after you have elevated yourself. It is a humbling experience. To be harshly reminded that you are made of the same human ingredients as the others that you may be (subconsciously) looking down on. But after digesting the humble pie, you also realize how liberating it is. To know that you are human. To know that because you are human, you will make mistakes. You will mess up (sometimes big time). There will be times when you will be wise and times when you will be reckless. To be reminded that you may have several badges of honour but there will also be some walks of shame. That you will make some great decisions and some terrible decisions.

"I am human. Nothing human is alien to me." I will forgive myself as often as I need to.

2020 Part 2:
The Different Faces of
Grief

I HAVE BEEN GRIEVING. For at least seven months.

It hasn't always been apparent to me that I am grieving. I do not struggle to get out of bed in the morning. I play with my daughters and laugh with my husband. I manage to make homecooked meals on various days of the week. I chat happily with my neighbours and hold conversations with mums and dads at the school gate. I give good lectures and the quality of my work has generally not been affected. I laugh. I smile. Indeed, I have several joyous days.

But when I look back at 2020, it is also apparent that I have been grieving – in subtle, but still painful ways. The inability to observe my five daily prayers, even though I am at home all day. Promising friends that I would return phone calls that I find myself repeatedly unable to make. Failing to respond to urgent emails. Starting important conversations that I do not finish. Failing to wish my family and friends a Merry Christmas and a Happy New Year.

I am grieving.

I am grieving the loss of lives – relatives, friends, friend's relatives, friend's friends. Even strangers. I am grieving the loss of income – cancelled contracts, reduced funding, unrelenting bills. I am grieving the loss of pockets of wellbeing – being unable to see our families in Uganda as earlier planned, seeing a lot less of our families in the UK, not being able to gather with my lady friends – the women of Barnett Road – to drink from their fountains of wisdom and be comforted by their graceful compassion. I am grieving injustices in our society. And I am grieving the "could bes" for my children – Level X of swimming by summer 2020, personal best at the park run by September 2020, play dates and birthday parties. Seemingly small, yet still, treasured collections.

We don't like to talk about grief.

In fact, we are generally uncomfortable around negative emotions. When a child cries, we tell them to stop crying. When they lash out in anger, we scold them. We teach them at a very early age that they should suppress their emotions because we generally do not know how to be around big feelings. When a person quickly recovers from a loss or an injury, we praise them for their strength and bravado. When they take a long time to recover, we avoid them or find ways of letting them know that they should "get over it". Some people have been through worse things, we remind them. When someone is suffering from pain or loss, we quickly direct their attention to the things that they should be grateful for. We have learnt to shout loudly so that we do not have to listen to our fears. We position ourselves in the limelight so that we do not have to face our darkness. We glorify happiness and stigmatize sadness, forgetting that they are equal parts of being human.

No one of course, in their right mind, openly embraces grief, sadness and the things that look like them. But the silence around them, the shame and stigma attached to them, deny us access to a core part of our humanity. What has made it possible for me to walk through the dark alleys of 2020 has been an ability to honour pain and sit with the disappointments that have accompanied the various losses. Because I have allowed myself to feel pain, I have also been able to recognize the most basic and yet most meaningful connections that have made these past seven months worthwhile, in spite of the darkness. Sitting on the carpet with my husband and daughters figuring out a puzzle. Cuddling in bed at the end of the day to read a chapter of a book. Speaking with my sisters and goofing around with my brothers. Listening to my mother narrate stories of things that we had never talked about in the past. My neighbours, once again, have crystallized my faith in the sanctity of community. The exchanges on the street WhatsApp group – where people offer to add items to their shopping lists in case someone is having trouble booking a home delivery slot or is not able to go to the shops. The people who cook meals for the sick, bake cakes to collect donations for the homeless, and give and share gently used items, costumes for Nativity plays and phone contacts for handymen.

Thanks to inspiration from my friends Olive and Nelly, I have also found a new way in which to connect with myself. Every weekday, at approximately 6am, I put on my trainers, throw on a coat and go for a long walk. These walks have been my meditation and medication. They have given me time to think about ways in which I could have been a more compassionate mother and ways in which I could have been a more understanding wife. They have allowed me to let tears of pain flow down my face and let in the joy of listening to birdsong. I have written sentences for book chapters and lined up arguments for academic papers. I have patted myself on the back for the things that I have done right and forgiven myself for the mistakes that I have made.

As I walk through 2021, my hope is that I can build more meaningful relationships. That I pick up the phone to call a dear one instead of being in a rush to mechanically respond to a WhatsApp message. That I stop and look at my daughters when they ask for my attention and think about the intentions behind my various actions. That when I ask people how they are, I take interest in truly knowing what they are experiencing. That I make the time for those who need me and share of the various gifts that I have been blessed with. That I practice compassion consistently, resist the temptation to judge others and continue to be aligned to my purpose. Lastly, I hope that I give myself (and others) as much permission to grieve my pain as I do celebrate my (and their) joy.

Men and Women

Traditionally, among the Baganda, when a girl reached the age of puberty, to avoid the risk of her engaging in premarital sex and getting pregnant, her *ssenga* (paternal aunt), was tasked with identifying a suitable spouse for her. Before getting married, the young woman would stay with her *ssenga*, who would educate her on a number of things including her duties as a wife, how to conduct herself in public as a married woman, general hygiene and the importance of patience during times of adversity. The groom-to-be, if he was a young and unmarried man, was advised by his elder male relatives on the importance of providing for his family, his responsibilities as the head of the household and the need for patience during times of adversity. At the introduction/ marriage ceremony (*kwanjula*), the man and his family were tasked with explaining how they were going to take care of the young woman. On the morning that the young woman was going to leave her parents' home to live with her husband, she was pampered with a bath given to her by either her *ssenga* or her paternal grandmother. Marriage was not just a union between the man and the woman, but also a coming together of their two families.

A lot has changed over the years. As young women (particularly in urban areas) spend more time in school and go on to acquire post-secondary education, marriage is delayed. In fact, increasingly, for a number of educated urban women, marriage is no longer a priority. And yet, as my cousin Mujib often joked, "Everything we do – day in and day out – is for love. We live for love."

Even though our opportunities and aspirations as women have undeniably changed over the years, what is expected from us in many ways remains unchanged. Whether we have high-paying jobs or our own businesses, whether we live in high income countries or low income countries, we still undertake the bulk of unpaid work in the home. We are still, oftentimes, the primary carers for our children, elderly relatives and the sick. And while the women in my tradition continue to consult with *ssengas*, there is hardly any expectation on men to consult with male elders. Lately, the institution of the *ssenga* has become highly commercialised (in urban areas) with bridal showers being organized where a total stranger is paid to come and provide marital advice to the bride to be. Despite this commercialisation, the flavour of the core message remains the same: serve your man (with food and with A LOT of sex – the *ssengas'* fees also cover juicy details on the various kinds of moans and movements that are guaranteed to make your man stick); hold onto your man tightly – because by now you should have noticed that there are a lot more women than there are men; and do not divulge your marital issues (in other words, suffer in silence).

In many ways, we have it much better than our mothers and grandmothers did. Better access to education. More financial security. Better healthcare. In other ways, our mothers and grandmothers had it much better than we do. They had stronger roots and ties. Circles of accountability and networks of support.

Do We Have a New
Breed of Men?
Have Women Changed?

O R IS THIS WHAT they call growing up?
It is becoming increasingly common to hear the word divorce. To hear a woman complaining that the father of her children is not giving her any child support after they separate. To hear a man saying that he wants out of a relationship because of the stress he feels it causes him. It is no longer uncommon to hear young ladies boasting about the fact that they are independent women who do not need men in their lives. Or young men boasting about the fact that there are so many women to choose from. We seem to be living in times where people see each other as easily disposable and replaceable. I often find myself wondering: Do we have a new breed of men? Have women changed? Or is this what they call growing up?

One chilly winter evening, a group of friends and I met for one of our usual "Africans in the diaspora" get togethers. As is normally the case during such gatherings, we talk about a cocktail of things to match the assortment of food and drinks that accompany the meetings. We complain about our greedy politicians. We lament about the state of our healthcare systems. We talk about the drama in the lives of our local celebrities (some of whom we may know on a personal level). We share tips about where to get the most legit *matooke* (green bananas) or fresh beans (normally a store run by Indians or Nigerians). Naturally, we also talk about relationships. That chilly winter evening, one of my male friends said: "I miss women like my grandmother. She was in many ways the leader of the household and pretty much made most of the decisions. But she didn't need to be loud. She didn't need to look like she was in control. Yet as I grew older, I realized that she was pretty much the decision maker. However, in public, she let my grandfather feel like he was the head of the household. Women of these days are the complete opposite."

Since then, I have found myself pondering over what it means to be a "grandmother wife" and whether women should aspire to be "grandmother wives".

The "grandmother wife" is not loud but she is powerful. She is not forceful, but she is a force to reckon with. She is patient and she is wise. She might have been in the back garden most of the time but she was also at the forefront of many decisions. She is the opposite of today's woman. Today's woman is visible and can be loud. Some say she is bossy. She is often accused of being impatient.

Was the grandmother wife happy and content? Would she advise us to act the way she used to act? Should we be aspiring to go back to being grandmother wives when we have more rights than they did, better access to education and more financial independence? What attributes of the grandmother wife would serve us well today?

Of course, I do not have answers to these questions. I will say, however, that as a woman, I am exhausted. I am exhausted from seeing hardworking and respectable women being broken. I am tired of hearing women being told by society that they need to be "grandmother" wives when men are not being told that they need to be like their grandfathers. I am frustrated with a culture in which women are blamed and shamed and made to feel inadequate when men are frequently glorified simply for being male. I find it hypocritical that women are often told to speak with their *ssengas* when men are not told to speak with their *kojas* (uncles). It is exhausting that women are taking on a huge share of the financial burdens of households and yet continue to also carry the load of unpaid care work.

I recognize that this is a bit of a generalization. Of course, there are men who are doing better. There are men who are committed partners; men who are intimately engaged in the upbringing of their children; men who are advocates for women's rights. However, for the most part, society continues to glorify men at the expense of women. It romanticizes grandmother wives, forgetting that grandmothers often had few options.

I am old fashioned. Old fashioned in the sense that I value the family unit. But for this to work, men need to do better. We need to teach our sons that respect is earned, not inherited. We need to remind them that while there are plenty of women out there, there are also plenty of men. So it is really not about the numbers. It is about the quality and compatibility. It is about growing up and acknowledging that while we can dispose of relationships and each other, if we do not do the hard work of valuing each other, then we are always going to chase after shadows of happiness. We need to remind them about fairness. We need to let our daughters know that it is okay to speak up and speak loudly. And that it is okay to be without a man, especially if being with one means that they have to reduce themselves to fit into a man's fragile ego. We need to discourage shame – assure them that it is okay to choose formal work over being a housewife and that it is okay to choose to be a housewife without having to feel the need to explain oneself to a whole village.

If we are going to talk about grandmother wives, we are going to have unpack exactly what that meant. What was good about it? What can we borrow and what needs to be thrown out? And importantly, what was the responsibility of men then? What can today's men borrow from that and how can they improve it?

Dear Husband
(Part 1)

Dear husband
Today at Fatmah's *kwanjula*
My *ssenga* called me into the bedroom.
She said that she was concerned
I seemed to be slacking
On my duties as a wife.
She reminded me
That to keep a man
I needed to be diligent
And masterful.
She demonstrated all sorts of acrobatics
Moans and movements.
I looked away
Embarrassed to watch the display
On a woman of her age.

My girlfriends confirmed *ssenga*'s theories
They reminded me of our friend
Nakato

Whose fifty-seven-year-old husband
Found himself a fresh university student.
They warned me
"If you do not give him sex
He is going to look for it elsewhere."

What no one cared to find out
Is why I feel so sexless.
Because if they had asked
I would have told them
That sometimes
I am exhausted to the bone
From the burdens
Of ironing and cooking.
Making sure that two-year old Juma
Doesn't swallow those stones again,
Helping ten-year old Stella
With algebra,
All while trying
To respond to the urgent email
From my panicky boss.

If they had asked me
I would have told them
That if you took up
Some of the chores
I swear to you
I would have done
Bedroom gymnastics
Hanging from the living room chandelier.

If they had asked me
I would have told them
That if you had taken the time
To find out the cravings of my body
The things that turn me on
My waters would flow
Like the waters of the River Nile.

Dear husband
I found out about the other woman
And her six-year-old child
She didn't have to tell me
That you are the father
Of her son
That forehead doesn't lie.
When I confided in my friends
They reminded me
That they had warned me
If I had given you another child…
If I had stayed at home
Instead of taking that job…
If only I didn't
Complain so much…
Maybe then
You would have no need to meander.
Forgive my French
Dear husband
But I call that total crap.
An excuse of a man.

Dear husband
Today you looked at me
And told me that I had grown fat.
I saw the disgust on your face
Before you turned back to your phone.
The other day
You told me
That I had become undesirable
Nothing resembling the woman you had married.
That I, your seven-month pregnant wife
Had neglected my looks.
You joked about my big nose.
I looked again at your forehead
And landed on your nostrils
And decided
"Not today woman, not today.
You are above this."

Dear husband
Today am packing my bags
Heading back to my parents.
I have been warned
By the women in the Mothers' Union
That I will bring shame to my people
That at my age
I am no longer marriage material
They said: "*Guma.*
We have seen worse."
But you see, dear husband

My parents…
They didn't chase me from their home
In fact, they keep reminding me
Their home will always be my home
They keep reminding me
Of how proud of me they are
Proud of my achievements
Of the woman I have become.
It is time I went back
To be wrapped in their loving nest
To remember what it is like
To smile
To be tickled with laughter
To be appreciated
And valued
And oh!
What I would give
To get my voice back.

As for the women at the Mothers' Union
Well, they seem to have forgotten
That just last month
Maama Moses?
She was beaten to death
By her "darling husband".
And Maryam, while she is not beaten
She really is
As good as dead
Her beautiful smile is no more
Once a bag of confidence

Now a shadow of her past.
As for Mellissa
Well, where do I start?

SHOW ME YOUR PEOPLE

WHEN MY HUSBAND AND I decided that we were going to get married, as is tradition among the Baganda, a date was set for the meeting of the two families (the *kukyaala*). It was a small and intimate gathering held in my father's living room. My husband was accompanied by his father, his mother, his two elder brothers, his elder sister and a close family friend (who was well-known to my father). They took with them a handful of supplies as an offering to my family – milk, bread, sugar and rice. On my side of the family were my father, my mother, my father's wife, my elder sister, my *ssenga*, one of my paternal uncles and my mother's good friend. I was out of the country at the time and we had collectively decided that it would not make much (financial) sense for me to travel back home for this single meeting. I was, after all, ably represented by my family. My mother had requested me to be on standby should they need to consult me on anything.

While this is intended to be a crucial meeting among the Baganda, to be honest, I did not think much would come out of it. Because most traditional functions nowadays seem to be more about the glitter than the gist, I imagined that this was going to be one of those ceremonial box-ticking exercises where my parents would just be happy that I had found a man to marry me (I had been warned by a number of people that the combination of a law degree and a PhD did not make for good marriage material in a woman). Like any young lady who is eager to get married, I wanted all this official traditional stuff to be done and over with so that we could go on with our real (exciting) lives. My insecurities also meant that I constantly texted my husband-to-be – first to make sure that he had not changed his mind about the visit (and about marriage) and second, well… to just get on with our lives!

"We are running a little late. Still waiting for Hajji Abas" (the family friend).

"He's here now. On our way."

"Arrived."

The text messages kept coming in – in response to my nudges.

After that, there were no more text messages from him.

Luckily, there was my sister! My new informant!

I soon found out that things were getting a little tough. My father, in my opinion at the time, was just being ridiculous! He was asking all these questions: What were our plans? When did we intend to have the religious ceremony? Where did we plan to live after we got married? Were there any elders that we could consult when we experienced hardships in our marriage? What financial cushions did we have in place? What assurances could my husband-to-be's family give him that his daughter was going to be treated well? Did they know how much his daughter meant to him? How much he loved her?

When my father was not satisfied with some of the responses, he and his "clan" asked to be excused so that they could consult among themselves. They went away for what to me seemed like a gazillion years. "Things are tight. Your dad is tough" read the text message from my husband-to-be.

Being thousands of miles away, I was beginning to get nervous. Soon, that nervousness turned into anger. *Who did my father think he was? Was he there when we met? Was he the one going to live in this marriage? Did he know what it had taken for us to get to this point? Did he know how lucky I was that I was getting married to this man? That this man had chosen me? What if, because of his silly actions, my husband-to-be changed his mind about the marriage?*

Not once did it cross my mind to think: *Did my in-laws-to-be know how lucky they were that I was considering (okay, truthfully, that I had made up my mind a long time ago) getting married to their son? Did my husband know how lucky he was to have me? That I had chosen him? What if I changed my mind?*

It took me several years to fully understand the significance of that meeting. To understand that in that meeting, my husband and his family had been made to understand that:

- I am loved and treasured. My family was not desperate to get rid of me.

- I have a home to go back to, should I not be treated with the respect and dignity that I deserve.
- I have my people. My ride-or-die clan.
- My husband and his family were lucky to have me.

You see, as young women – and sometimes even as older women – we often think that someone is doing us a favour by marrying us. We squeal when the man finally says: "Okay, I will marry you", forgetting that we can also say: "Wait a minute. Let me also check with myself to see whether this works for me." And when we do get married, we try as much as possible to assimilate into the man's family, forgetting where we came from. We do not invest as much time in getting them to know our people as we do in trying to get to know (and be liked by) their people. We forget to show them that we come from places where we are loved, where we are cherished, where we are valued. And, if need be, where we shall be happily accepted back.

SO WHAT IF YOUR MAN
DOESN'T LOVE YOU?

I DON'T REMEMBER MY husband ever seriously telling me that he loves me. If he did, it was such a long time ago that I have no recollection of it. When he does say he loves me, it is normally as a joke, which is followed by laughter from both of us (and a look of amused confusion from our daughters). My husband doesn't give me roses on Valentine's Day. And for my birthday, he has to set a yearly reminder. Out of the blue, at about 12.03pm on my birthday, I receive a suspicious text message from him wishing me a happy birthday. Now that I think about it, I don't remember when he last bought me a present for my birthday. And then there is Mother's Day. When I once joked about him not getting me a present for Mother's Day, he said something about me not being his mother… LOL (The nerve, right)?

It goes without saying that we are not the kind of couple that you will find holding hands in public or making public declarations of love.

Pretty sad, eh?

Maybe.

But only if I ignore all the other things that he is and that he does. Only if I ignore the fact that he makes me laugh a lot of the time. Only if I ignore the fact that he may not bring me roses on Valentine's Day or buy me gifts on my birthday, but every time he sees something that he thinks I will like and which he can afford, he gets it for me (sometimes, it is just the newest flavour of Magnum ice cream). Only if I ignore the fact that he is my sounding board and a cheerleader for most of my aspirations. Only if I ignore the fact that sometimes, he serves as my moral compass. Only if I ignore the fact that our relationship may not be romantic, but it is a practical kind of happy where our equivalent of breakfast in bed is one of us telling the other that it is their turn to go downstairs and bring us tea. Only if I ignore the fact that some mornings, we spend hours in bed talking about aspects of life that we find fascinating such as the importance of community, lessons from our elders and building successful partnerships.

If you asked my husband whether he loves me, he will tell you that he doesn't know. He will say that he doesn't know because in his very logical and philosophical sense, he will say that he does not understand what love really means. So how can he profess something that he does not understand? He will tell you instead that he cares about me. That he respects me. That he appreciates the contribution that I make to our family. And he will probably not admit this in my presence, but he also knows that he has a pretty awesome wife.

Does this mean that we are living in paradise and have it all figured out? Obviously not. Like any relationship, there are moments. Difficult moments of dealing with difficult emotions. Moments of disappointment. Moments of frustration. Moments of hardship. Moments of awkward silences. Such, I have come to learn, are part of the fabric of living. The best that we can do during such moments is to learn how to handle them better. Learn how to be respectful of each other, even when we disagree. To remember the value that we add and the contribution that we make to each other. We don't always get it right. In fact, we are still very much a work in progress. But it is the other moments – of laughter, of being silly, of having deep conversations, that remind us why this relationship is precious.

For a young woman who was hopelessly romantic, I had to deal with the reality of being with a man whose affection manifests itself differently from what I see around me. I had to stop the comparison. To stop wanting our relationship to mirror those of others – whether in reality or in fiction. Now, as an academic researcher, I appreciate the value of doing comparative analyses. I appreciate the importance of learning from systems that are working well. But I also know that there is something terribly wrong with seeking to transplant a system from one location to another without taking into account the realities of the local context in which the transplant is being placed. The same can be said about relationships. It would be wrong for me to conclude that because my sister's husband always gets her a gift on her birthday, he cares about her more than my husband cares about me. To begin with, my husband does not even remember his own birthday! At least he makes an attempt by setting a reminder for mine! It would be wrong for me to insist that my husband should tell me that he loves me or portray his love by putting a picture of us on his Facebook profile just because that's what my friend's husband does.

Obviously, there's a lot that we can learn from comparison. We can learn how to communicate better by learning from those who do it well. We can learn patience. We can learn how to better support each other. We can learn how not to be treated.

But most times, instead of picking these lessons, we complicate our relationships with pressures of wanting to be seen to be in love. The outward display of affection. We fail to appreciate what we have before us because we are too busy trying to get endorsements about our relationships from other people. We compare our spouses with others and require them to do what we see other people's spouses do (in public). We want to achieve the bliss that we witness in other people's pictures on Instagram and Facebook, without truly understanding their journeys and the authenticity of those journeys. We put ourselves under pressure to be seen to be living "the life" instead of actually tuning in and connecting to the life.

Until we find our own happy, until we keep out the noise and turn off the flashlights, we shall continue chasing after shadows of happiness and ignore the beauty that is right before us.

WHAT HAPPENS AFTER HE PUTS A RING ON IT?

I WAS FIDDLING WITH my wedding ring the other day and it got me thinking back on the day that my husband and I got married. The two of us have always been practical people. Okay, that is a bit of a lie. For as long as I have known him, my husband has always been a practical person. I, on the other hand, did and do occasionally travel to *la la land*. I have always been a "ring girl". When I was an undergraduate student at Makerere University, I had a whole collection of cheap rings in different colours. I dreamt of the day when I would have a proper high carat gold ring like the ones I saw in Argos catalogues (Argos, of course, being one of the poshest places that I knew at the time). Like many young ladies, I also dreamt of the day when my then boyfriend would surprise me with a proposal on bended knee – just like in the movies. I toyed with different versions of the proposal. *Maybe he will do it in front of my siblings. Maybe he will take me to dinner in a cosy and expensive restaurant and the waiter will uncover the dessert bowl only for me to find a little black box. Maybe it will be just the two of us taking a lazy walk through a park. Maybe he will send a little boy to walk up to me with a little box while he hides behind a tree or something.*

Well … none of that happened. My husband did not propose. At some point, after holding my breath for what seemed like eternity, I brought up the topic of marriage. He wasn't too enthusiastic about it. He didn't immediately say yes. But somewhere along the way, he must have agreed. Because one day, he called me and said: "So, will you still want a ring when we get married? What are your finger dimensions?" Talk about romantic! Anyway, I was not going to let the absence of romanticism rain on my parade. I was going to pretend that he proposed and surprised me with a ring.

As I walked around jewellery shops in Vancouver trying to get my finger dimensions (because believe it or not, these questions were asked over the phone from oceans away), I psyched myself up about the fact that I was finally going to wear legit bling!

Until I saw the ring.

To put it mildly, the ring that I got was far from those that blind the eyes. If you are going to look for the stone on the ring, you will require a bit of mining expertise (I am still trying to find it myself!). I recall with amusement the utter disappointment on the face of one of my husband's romantic friends. When we had just got married, his friend came walking excitedly towards me: "Let me see your ring!" he said, fidgeting like an excited little child. I put my hand out. "Oh, it's nice", he added, unable to hide his crushed feelings. He did look a little confused.

Instead of the bling, the real stone that laid the foundation for our marriage was one of the first questions that my husband-to-be asked me when we decided that we were going to get married: "What happens when we have a disagreement? Who in your family should I talk to?" He then went ahead to tell me the people in his family that I should talk to if we failed to resolve a dispute. These questions sobered me. Even though I had seemingly been thinking about marriage for a much longer time than him, I realized that what I had really been thinking about was the wedding, living happily ever after and being called *mukyala gundi*. I had not seriously thought about what marriage meant.

He, on the other hand, had been thinking about what commitment meant. If he was going to commit to something this serious, then he needed to know what we would do when we hit hard bottoms – as we inevitably have done over the years.

Even though I didn't receive the kind of bling that I was hoping for, I have, over the years, received various "rings" from him. Rings that have put into better perspective what a union means. These rings have included having a partner that I can speak with about my dreams. They have included someone who respects me and who respects my family. They have included someone who protects my image in front of his family. They have included being with someone who does not buy me gifts on my birthday or flowers on Valentine's Day, but who expresses how much he cares for me in various other practical ways. The rings have also been crystallized by two precious little girls who many times do our heads in but who are a source of abundant joy and endless laughter.

But the rings have not been all about glitter and glam. They have also included discussions that have been so difficult that our hearts hurt. They have included going through moments of doubt about the survival of our marriage. They have included disappointing each other and sometimes, even causing pain to each other.

Through all these hiccups, the questions – "What happens when we have a disagreement? Who in your family should I talk to?" – have provided the groundwork with which to resolve disputes. They have enabled us to turn to the people we love, respect and trust to act as our sounding boards during those moments when our own reasoning is encumbered.

The other day when I was fiddling with my ring, I thought about the multiple layers of its invisible carats.

GRATITUDE

I WALK INTO THE house in the evening. My husband has been at home with the kids all day. I find toys littered everywhere. There's a pile of laundry on the sofa. It looks like the girls have been playing with the laundry because some of the clothes are on the floor and I see a food stain on one of my dresses that has an uncanny resemblance to the patch on one daughter's unwashed mouth. The carpet is messy. It is past our usual dinner time but the kids have not had their shower.

I have two options.

Option One: I start to slowly boil on the inside, my mind racing. *What have they been doing all day? Who is going to clean up this mess? What happened to timekeeping and sticking with routine? What …* I get a headache just looking at all the chaos. I open my mouth and complain about the mess. I complain about how late it is. I complain about the fact that the kids have not even had their bath. I complain about the clothes on the floor and the twin stains. I complain.

Version 2 of Option One: I become passive aggressive. I do not complain but my actions are loud. My silence is even louder. I aggressively pick up the laundry and fold it with clenching teeth. I look at the man and his two children (because, in this moment, they are not my relatives) and wonder how people can live like this. *Who bred them? What planet did they come from?* I say a curt hello. I walk upstairs with the heap of laundry, stamping my feet on the creaky stairs.

Option Two: I walk in and start thinking in my head: "If I had been home today, by now, the kids would have had their bath, their toys would be tucked away and we would be having dinner." Sigh. But since I was not home all day, "Hello! How was your day everyone?!" I smile, allowing the girls to fall into my arms, smudging the food stains onto my tired dress. I ask my husband if he would like me to take the girls up for a quick shower.

I could complain about the things that haven't been done. Or I could notice the things that have been done. I could start by appreciating that my husband has been home with the kids all day. They have been in a safe environment and are clearly well fed. They have had a fantastic time turning the house upside down.

And since I checked both my mouth and my attitude, I soon find out that while the house is a mess, I smell a sweet aroma from the kitchen. The kids had a nap and fruit after their nap. I also find out that while the laundry is lying around, there's another load of laundry running in the washing machine. I smile.

I am grateful.

Being the smart mouth that I can be, my default was normally some version of Option One. It normally revolved around the kids and the fact that the regime of a routine that I had put in place was being messed up. Invariably, it resulted in anger, awkward silences and, eventually, apologies (from me). I started gravitating towards Option Two and here is what I have learnt along the way.

Gratitude works wonders. Acknowledging the effort of someone's actions instead of unpicking what they have not done makes them want to do more. Human beings thrive on validation. The fact that they are seen. When, for example, I get an email from a client thanking me for the way I handled an assignment, I am motivated to do better. But it is also good for the heart of the giver. When we are grateful, we tend to smile more. We tend to appreciate more the small things in life. And life really is a collection of small things.

It is important to remember that we are all different. We prioritize things differently. We often forget and expect others to do things exactly the way we would have done them. In fact, sometimes, consciously or subconsciously, we expect others to do things in the order in which we would have done them. We need to remember that we function differently. I have a good friend, for example, who prioritizes meals over a clean house. Her husband, on the other hand, would rather have a clean house than a meal in his stomach. Luckily, they recognize their differences and are employing their energy towards their priorities. They get to have food and a clean house. Happy household!

Even though we frequently talk about the importance of diversity, particularly in the workplace, we forget to embrace diversity in our private spaces. We forget that embracing our differences can lead to healthier and happier homes.

We can start by appreciating the things that others (whether our relatives or those who work in our homes) have done, instead of obsessing over the things that they have not done. The fact that someone has been at home all day with our children. The fact that we come back to a happy household. Or we find a warm meal or a warm embrace waiting for us.

These are the little blessings that I am learning to identify and acknowledge.

DEAR HUSBAND (PART 2)

Dear husband
Try not to act surprised
When you come back home later today.
Nakato is here
With little Tendo and Kirabo
Their luggage in a small suitcase.
She should have packed her bags earlier, she says
But like many women
She thought and hoped
Prayed and stayed
Trusting that things would get better.
First, he slapped her
And apologized profusely
The next time
He grabbed her hand so tightly
He left a huge mark on her wrist
He apologized again
And apparently even cried.
But today

When he pushed her into the wall
Not caring that she was carrying a child inside her
Not caring that little Tendo
Was right there watching
She walked out.
Before walking out
She said to him
"Not once did I see my father lifting his hand
To hit my mother.
This is not love."
I looked at her
My heart bursting with pride
Our baby
Standing up against
An excuse of a man
Even though we know
How much she still loves him.

Dear husband
A pleasant thing happened today.
As I was combing through Maama Salim's market stall
Trying to find the ripest watermelon
For our guests later today
Sarah, our daughter-in-law
Came running to me and squeezed me in a tight hug
I wondered if she was alright.
She stepped back
Looked deep into my eyes
Her own eyes dipped in emotion
And said

"Thank you for raising a good man
A man who respects me
A man who is not intimidated by my accomplishments
A man who supports me
Cheers me on
And sees me as a partner
Nothing like my first husband
Who stepped all over me
Like I was a doormat."
I said to her
A generous beam spread across my face
"Well, I can only take part credit for that.
Mwami set a great example."
We embraced again.

Dear husband
Wasn't it wonderful
When the children came to visit today
Bringing along their children
And their spouses?
Don't you feel content
When they call you
Just to say hello?
Tell you how much they love you?
When they seek your counsel
On relationships
On business decisions
And on raising children?
The other day
Sula and I laughed

About when you took part in that sack race
Even though the other dads
Were almost half your age
Admittedly
I was scared
That you would get a heart attack
But I saw how happy
Little Sula was
Even though quite embarrassed
When you eventually came in miles after the rest.

Dear husband
It must feel good
That at 70
You have me here with you
Now that our children are gone
Now that your youth is gone
Now that your teeth are gone
Now that the flashlights
Of the dancehalls have dimmed
Now that the temporary pleasures
Of following lustful desires
Have finally revealed
Their emptiness
To your friends
Amos and Kamara and Mustafa
Remember
How they always made fun of you?
Calling you a "goody-two-shoes"
Joking about how you acted

Like the woman of the house?
Telling you that you were not man enough
Because you had no side chick?
I wonder what they think now
As they languish
In the silence of their material possessions
And the absence of connection
Uninteresting even for side chicks.
What is it they used to say?
"YOLO"?

Dear husband
They say that there are no good men
That all men are dogs
That all men cheat
That handsome men are unfaithful
And rich men
Have no time for their families.
I point them to
Mr and Mrs Kakembo
Celebrating their fifty-eighth anniversary.
I introduce them to Engineer Odong
Who tells them the story
Of how he loved his wife with a fierce passion
Even when he was ridiculed
For not being a man
For staying with a barren wife.
I tell them about Mr Twinomugisha
Who takes great pride
In mingling *kalo*

And marinating chicken
Telling the same joke
Twenty years later
About how Mrs Twinomugisha
Burnt that chicken
On the first day of their marriage.
I show them the youthful Dr Ssali
Who spends his days
Out of the operating room
Playing *tapo* and *kwepena*
With five-year old Nambi
Teaching her how to make *dole ze byaayi*
All while singing
Ffe tuli embata ento.

But that is searching too far, I say,
Right here with me
Is a man
Who for the past thirty years
Has treated me like a queen
A man
Who still gives me the shivers
Who makes me laugh
And makes me smile
Who makes me feel like a child
Who is naughty
And wise
Funny and kind
Whose love and commitment
Renew our marriage vows

Every single day.

There are good men out there,
I say.

Dear women
Don't let the bad ones
Turn you into a cynic
And certainly
Don't let the bad ones
Make you settle for less.
For then
You would much rather
Glow in your own presence.
Because woman
You are worthy
You are beautiful
You are amazing
You deserve the best.

As for you dear husband
What kind of man
Do you choose to be?

2020 Part 3:
Do You Ask for
What You Need in a
Relationship?

My sister-friend, Annette, who is also in many ways my unpaid relationship counsellor, once told me that one of the things that she discovered after several years of marriage was the importance of asking for what she needs in a relationship. This, she explained, takes different forms. For example, instead of waiting for her husband to surprise her with a birthday present that she might not like or would end up not using, she had learnt to let him know some of the things that she wanted. Instead of waiting for him to figure out that he would need to be at home with the children when she had an important appointment, she consulted with him about his schedule and let him know what her plans were. Instead of waiting for him to prioritize family dinners over work, she would tell him what time they would be having dinner and let him know that it would be nice if he joined them.

I wasn't married when we first had this conversation (we have had it several times since), but I remember thinking: *Shouldn't we leave some room for our spouses to surprise us? Wouldn't an adult be wise enough to figure some of these things out without you having to tell them? Would I not seem needy on the one hand and demanding on the other hand to make some of these requests?* Like many young women, as Annette was telling me this, I secretly thought that my relationship would be different. It would be special. I would not need to communicate my needs and expectations because my husband would feel them. The fact that I was a good, respectful and hardworking woman, meant that my husband would be looking for every opportunity to outdo me. We were soulmates who would figure out by osmosis and telepathy what the needs of the other person were. We would be each other's mirror. Surely, marriage should not be that complicated!

I could provide many examples of where I was proved wrong. But let me talk about the most recent one. In March 2020, when schools in the UK closed because of a nationwide lockdown caused by the coronavirus pandemic, I assumed that the two adults in the house (namely, my husband and I), would automatically figure out that we would each have to pick up many more child-care hours. I was wrong.

Week One: My husband continues to operate as if it is business as usual. He does his work-work and then chips in with the work that he normally does in the home – as if the children are still in school. I, on the other hand, am now a full-time working mother. I am the key worker, PE teacher, referee (sibling fights can be quite brutal in this area code – including things like, "You looked at me like this." Go figure), canteen lady for snack time, core subjects' teacher and dinner lady. All of this is in addition to the fact that I have work assignments to complete. *My husband is a reasonable man. He will soon figure out that he needs to do more.*

Right?

Wrong.

Week Two: Monday ... Tuesday ... *Wait – this is beginning to look a lot like Week One – only worse.* I am still dinner lady, canteen lady, referee, art teacher, PE teacher (now they also want to do Jaime's yoga – first world problems) and the instructor for the new baking classes because "Mummy we saw this amaaaaazing recipe!" "Oh, and Mummy, when are you going to do our hair? I want mine to be like Elsa's."

What does Mummy do? I start to *kusiba sumbusa* (direct translation: "tying samosa". Okay, making a face). If he sees my *sumbusa*, he will figure out that there is trouble in paradise.

Right?

Wrong.

By Wednesday, my *sumbusa* is from Brighton, United Kingdom to my father's village in Butambala, Uganda. I am not smiling any more. I am mostly mute – apart from grudgingly responding to the questions which are directed at me and noisily bumping into the sofa as I carry the laundry upstairs to demonstrate just how burdened I feel. I am ill-tempered.

Week Two, Friday: I prepare to go and have a word with Mr (because now he is no longer "darling husband"). Before walking into his new office, I wear my military combat face. I am going to attack.

And then I remember: *This approach has never got me anywhere. It always leads to a deadly silence. We both get into defence mode.* I soften my facial features, relax my shoulders and prepare to engage in a conversation instead of a war. I open the door to the office and say: "Do you have a few minutes?" He nods yes. "We need to figure out some kind of schedule of how we are going to work around the kids."

His response? "Okay."

We sit down and draw up a plan. One year later, this plan still serves us, with some occasional adjustments.

These are a few things I have learnt over the years:

Women and men think differently (Mars, Venus, Think Like a Man etc., etc.). In this case, while I was busy thinking about how we were going to organize our schedules around the kids, my husband was busy thinking about how we were going to survive financially.

I have learnt to give my husband the benefit of the doubt. To remember that he is not the enemy. Silence is the enemy. Communication is thus key. I do not get this right all the time. But I am increasingly discovering the gems in good communication, including the importance of communicating one's needs.

I am learning to ask for my needs. Some may think it sounds needy or aggressive. That was my thinking too for many years. But we all have needs. Man and woman are better off putting them on the table for discussion.

Silence breeds resentment. Silence, when you are carrying a heavy burden in your heart, is not really golden. It just makes you more resentful.

I have no intention of being super woman. I long ago gave up the need to be the perfect wife and the perfect mum. The one who smiles even when I am hurting. The one who doesn't need help. The one who can maintain a sparkling house, freshly baked cookies, *matooke mu ndagala*, all while dressed in heels and with the perfect hairdo. Nope. I am quite content being an amazingly ordinary woman who needs a hand. Constantly.

Obviously, we didn't get to this point with the one trial in 2020 lockdown. This has been work in progress for many years. And it is still work in progress.

Without really being conscious about the impact of my actions on that day in March 2020, I later realized that there was another message that these new negotiations had sent to my daughters. They got to learn that my work as a woman also mattered. That I could love them more than anything in the world but also choose to spend some time on work that nourished me. That when they grow up, this may remind them that as women, they should also exercise their options. That if they decide to get married or live with a man, they should not give up on their dreams. I know that I would be quite unhappy if I was forced to make that choice. And I am glad that through this one seemingly small thing, I am able to model these options for them. Now, when I ask them to close the door behind them on a day or time that they are supposed to be with their father, they say, "Oh yes, today we are with *taata*."

What Happens When
We Ask?

WHAT HAPPENS WHEN, INSTEAD of passing judgement, we ask: I wonder what they are going through? What are their hidden scars? What are they struggling with?

What happens when, instead of failing to try, for fear of being rejected, we ask: is there any chance that we could explore option A or B or C? What can we learn from this process?

What happens when, instead of wearing tough faces and piling on resentment, we ask for the things that we want in a relationship?

What happens when, instead of imposing our ideas and solutions on others, we ask: how may I serve you? What is it that you need me to do to make you feel better?

What happens when, instead of dismissing those who do things differently from us, we ask: what could I learn from them? What is the message in their message?

We don't seem to ask frequently enough. We miss out on opportunities because we are afraid of rejection or too proud to be thought of as needy. Afraid of what the answer will be when we make a proposal. We stop growing and learning because we lack the courage to pose questions.

I find that when we ask, we unveil our shared humanity. When we fail to ask, we break the lines of communication. We close the doors of reconciliation and bury the hope born through curiosity.

MOTHERHOOD

Your children are not your children.
They are the sons and daughters of Life's longing for itself.
They come through you but not from you
And though they are with you yet they belong not to you.
Kahlil Gibran, 'On Children', **The Prophet**

THESE ARE THE THOUGHTS that ran through my mind when I had a miscarriage: *Will I ever conceive again? What if we are not compatible? What if I keep miscarrying? What if he leaves me? What if I can never bear children?*

Now that I have children, I find myself asking: *Am I a good enough mother? Will my children grow up to be happy adults? Will they approve of the choices that I made for them? Will they think that I failed them? How do I protect them?*

I need to keep reminding myself: *I am doing the best that I can with what I have. My mother did the best that she could with what she had. Every mother is doing the best that they can with what they have.*

FELLOW WOMAN.
ABOUT THE
MISCARRIAGE? ... I KNOW...

Fellow woman.
I know.
About the miscarriage.
And I sympathize.

I know.
About the harsh feeling of coldness in the womb
After experiencing the warmth of the body preparing to
carry child.

I know.
About the rudeness with which the body seems to be slowly
shutting down.
Full breasts collapsing back to normal.
Morning sickness sneakily disappearing.
No more feeling sleepy at odd hours.
No more craving for odd combinations of food.

I know.

About trying to convince yourself that it can't be a miscarriage.

"It's just spotting," you tell yourself.

And desperately clutch onto the fact that spotting is common in pregnancy.

"So maybe if I don't go to the toilet, it will stop.

Or maybe I should go to the toilet to confirm that it has stopped."

Except, it doesn't stop.

The thick clots of blood start to come out of you.

Each clot feeling like parts of a tiny body that could have been.

I know.

About the physical pain.

Raw.

It moves from the heart to the womb and right back to the heart.

Stop!

Please….

Stop…

I know.

About the guilt.

Even when the doctor says that it's nothing that you did.

Many women miscarry, he says,

For reasons that we don't fully understand.

Still, you think to yourself

"If only I had taken it easy."
"If only I hadn't walked too much."
"If only I hadn't taken that swim that morning."
"If only I hadn't drunk too much ginger tea."
"If only…"

I know.
About the fear and anxiety.
"What does this mean for the future?"
"Will I ever get pregnant again?"
"And if I do, will I be able to carry my baby to term?"

I know.
About the silence.
Because to talk about it may be a curse.
You may jinx yourself.
Words, after all, have power.
"I will heal and then try again next time."
"I will not share the news."

I know.
About the rude awakening.
How can life change in the split of a second?
"How can I experience such thrill one minute and such
agony the next?"

I know.
That the few close friends and family who know about
the miscarriage
Will tell you that all will be well.

And seeing as you have now joined the club,
Some will now find it fit to share their experiences
As a way of comforting you and giving you hope.
A part of you thinks: "They can speak about it because
they now have children."
But their speaking about it won't necessarily take the
pain away.
It will not necessarily take the anxiety away.

I still thought you should know that I know, fellow
woman.
Because I too experienced it.
I embrace you in a prayer of empathy and hope.

What Do Our Children Lose Out on When We Overprotect Them?

O NE DAY, I RECEIVED an email informing me that my daughter Mirembe had won a prize in a contest that she and her sister, Kirabo, had participated in. At the time of entering the contest, I had informed them that many children around the city would be participating in the contest and so, while we would do our very best, there was no guarantee that they would win. Frankly, having never really won anything in such competitions, I didn't think that they would win. But the contest involved going on a scavenger hunt around Brighton city, which meant that it would be a good way to kill the hours of a Saturday afternoon (and tire them out so that they go to bed early!)

When I received the news that Mirembe had won, I was super excited. My excitement was, however, short-lived. My mind was immediately directed to a ping-pong of questions: how would I break the news to Kirabo (who is just a year older) that only her sister had won, when they had put in an equal amount of effort? Would she, at such a tender age, be able to understand that this had nothing to do with her ability? Should I tell them that they had both won? Should I give away the prize so that we didn't have to deal with the heartbreak that would surely result from Kirabo finding out the truth?

I quickly consulted my younger sister, Didi, and my husband. Didi was very clear about the fact that she did not want to be involved in anything that resulted in breaking her little girl's heart. And anyway, she added, this is really not the thing to use to teach them life lessons. Not when they had both worked hard at it. There would be other opportunities for lessons. She even used a few Luo words to emphasize her point. My husband, with his characteristic inability to sugar-coat things, said: "Tell them the truth. Mirembe won. That doesn't mean that Kirabo lost. She just wasn't lucky this time round. That's life. Sometimes you win. Sometimes you don't."

The prize arrived. Even though I had made up my mind that I would tell them the truth, I was nervous when they came back home from school that evening. They saw the prize. The following conversation ensued:

Kirabo: "Wow! Did you buy us a new scooter?"

Nervous me: "No. You remember the competition we took part in?"

Kirabo: "Yes! We won?!"

Nervous me (barely breathing): "Not exactly. You remember when I said that we may win, or we may not win? And that maybe one person would win?"

Kirabo: "Yes. Who won?"

Nervous me (heart about to burst out): "Remember what I said. That it really doesn't matter who wins? That if one of you won you could share it, just like you share other things?"

Kirabo: "Yes… But Mummy! Who won?!"

Nervous (almost dead) me: "Uuuummmmm…"

Husband: "Mirembe won."

Kirabo: "Oh. Okay!"

Nervous me: "But it doesn't really matter. Remember how you two share all your stuff? So, this is sort of like you both won?"

Kirabo: "Maama, you know that it is okay that Mirembe won? I am actually happy for her. And anyway, sometimes she wins and sometimes I win."

Confused me: "Oh, okay."

Mirembe: "Yes, Maama. I am also happy for other children when they are on the bench of brilliance even when I am not on the bench of brilliance. Sometimes it is their turn. Sometimes it is my turn."

Confused me: "Oh, okay."

Mirembe (shaking her head vigorously): "Yes! And I will share with Kirabo!"

There it was. My children were reminding me that we do not have to have it all. That someone's possession of something does not mean that I lack. That when someone wins, it does not mean that I have lost. That we all have our turns to shine. That sometimes it will be my turn to be on the bench of brilliance and other times it will be another person's turn. That there is enough to go around – to share.

But it also got me thinking: what life lessons do our children lose out on when we seek to overprotect them?

I thought about past incidents when I had tried to protect them. Fearing to say no to them because I was afraid that it would hurt their feelings. Not allowing them to take risks because I feared that they would get hurt in the process. Lying to them because I thought that the truth would be too painful for their little hearts to bear. Doing things for them because I feared that if I did not, they would think that I did not love them.

That day, they taught me a lesson. Our children are more insightful than we think. Our children are more resilient than we think. Our children are more intelligent than we think. Our children can handle the truth. We can provide a safe and enabling environment for them. But we also need to let them experience what the real world is like. And if they get bruised in the process, at least we are there to offer Band Aid.

What Do We Teach Our Children When We Suffer From "the Disease to Please"?

SOME MONTHS AGO, I was walking my daughters to school along with a friend, who was also walking her daughter. I casually mentioned to my friend that I was running late for a meeting and would need to run off the minute I dropped each of the girls off at their class doors. As we approached the school gate, my friend kindly offered to take one of my daughters, who is in the same class with her daughter. I turned to my daughter and asked:

"Would you like to go with Stella and Marion?"

It must have been quite abrupt for her. Or maybe she just did not want to go with them on that day. She did not say no. But I saw the disappointed frown on her face. So, I said, "That's okay. Mummy will drop you off."

In what I assume was an attempt to please me, she quickly changed her mind and facial expression and said, "It's okay, Mummy. I will go with them."

I said, "That's okay, my dear. I will take you to your class. I can see you want to go with Mummy today."

I thanked my friend, a weak smile on my face. As if to apologize. Even though I felt like I had done the right thing by my daughter, I was concerned about what my friend would think. Would she think that my daughter did not like her? Would she be offended by the fact that my daughter did not want to go in with them? Should I send her a text message to explain that my daughter actually really likes her, and maybe apologize for what happened?

As I took the phone out to send the text message, my inner voice asked: *but what are you apologizing for Jalia? Does your daughter not have the right to say no? What message will you be sending your daughters if you teach them to put other people's feelings above their own?*

I did not send the text message.

Another day, we went to the park. I was sitting on a bench reading a book when Mirembe came to me and said that one of the boys was frightening her because he was making a scary face and uttering scary noises. A few minutes later, Kirabo also came, telling me something similar. They asked if they could sit with me. I said yes and added that they should listen to their feelings whenever they felt unsafe. I looked at the boy's mother, who was sitting on another bench about 100 metres away. I wondered whether she was offended that my daughters did not want to play with her son. I felt like smiling the apologetic smile. Instead, I cuddled my daughters in a warm embrace and avoided looking at her.

I tell these stories because I have often suffered from what Oprah calls "the disease to please". The fear of offending others – even when I am right. The need to make sure that others approve of me. That people know that I am a good person. Ignoring my feelings because I do not want to offend. I want to please. I want to be liked. I want to make people feel happy.

But what does this do to me? And what does it do to my children?

What does it do to our children when we care more about the feelings of adults (even when misplaced) than we care about their own feelings? What does it do to our children when we force them to smile for a picture that they do not want taken (just because we want to post it on social media)? What does it do to them when we force them to stop crying just because there are other people who are uncomfortable being around big emotions? What do we teach them when they don't want to hug Aunt Miriam or Uncle Wasswa, but we push them to do so anyway (because we do not want Aunt Miriam or Uncle Wasswa to be offended)? What messages do our seemingly small actions teach our children when they encounter bigger things?

Do you Take Note of How Your Unexamined Fears Affect Your Child's Confidence?

Т HE FIRST CUE SHOULD have been when my five-year daughter old said: "Maama, I didn't say I am not interested in learning. I just said I don't feel like doing it now!", an exasperated look on her face.

There were other cues. Like the time when she said: "Maama, I know how to read these words. But I am tired!" But the one that really hit home was when I was teaching her Maths and I wanted her to count without using sticks or objects (*because surely, how would an almost six-year-old learn how to add 1005 and 2567 if she had to keep using objects?*).

The following conversation ensued:

Me: "You need to learn to count without objects."

Daughter: "But in class we use objects like Lego and colours."

Me: "But what if you have to count a big number like fifty plus fifty?"

Daughter: "I would still use Lego. We have sooooooo many Lego pieces in class!"

Me: "What if it was a bigger number like 150 plus 200?"

Daughter: "Maama! We have all those Lego pieces in class! Seriously!"

Me: "What if it was like a million plus a million?"

Daughter (looking at me like the crazy woman that I was): "Maama, you realize that am not at Stringer?" (Dorothy Stringer being a secondary school).

That is when it hit me. *What was I doing to this beautiful child?*

Let me provide some context.

We had just come to the end of the school year. We had received our report cards – for reception class. I was okay with her report card. Until I found out that she had not performed as well as some of her peers.

One mum-friend: "Oh, mine got above expected in Maths, Reading and Writing. They got expected in behaviour and understanding the world."

Another mum-friend: "Mine got above expected in everything, apart from behaviour."

Another mum-friend: "Mine too!"

These were all innocent statements being made by mums during a casual conversation. I played it cool on the outside. But on the inside, panic mode had been turned on full blast. I thought back to the specifics of our report card. *What if she is not smart enough? What if she doesn't get into a good secondary school? What if she always stays behind her peers? What if things just get worse? What if I fail as a parent? OMG! OMG! OMG! What if? What if? What if?!*

Never mind that my daughter had just finished reception class. RECEPTION CLASS. It didn't matter that I had read and listened to a lot of research about the growth mindset. It didn't matter that I knew that we had not put in enough hours because as a full-time working mother, I was tired at the end of a working day and my precious little girl was tired after spending the rest of her day at an after-school club. It obviously didn't matter that she was just in reception. It didn't matter that I knew that she had done the best that she could with the tools that I had handed her. It didn't matter that I knew that she was better than her peers at some other things.

What mattered was the report card. We were going to set the record straight. We were going to show them (the teachers, other parents, her peers, whoever) that we were clever. And we were going to employ a military regime in doing so. We were going to learn Mathematics (to above expected), English (to above expected), Science (above expected), Geography … you get the drift. We would also be perfect at swimming, gymnastics and cover all those other sneaky little things that the education system thought that we couldn't decode.

And so, my daughter said: "Maama, I didn't say that I am not interested. I just said I don't feel like doing it now!" (Exasperated).

I thought that I had heard her. I thought that I had

listened. But how easy is it to relax as a parent when you have a report card to remind you of the differences?

On the other hand, how easy is it for our children to learn when we are in a constant state of panic and comparison.

And so, I ask myself: How often do you take note of how your unexamined fears affect your child's confidence?

This is some of what I have learnt along the way:

Children are great decoders. We can try to disguise our panic and disappointment as much as we want. Our children are still able to sense when fear and disappointment creep in. Like when my daughter says: "Maama, I don't like when you do that." I ask, feigning innocence: "Do what?" She responds: "When you do that thing with your face when I get something wrong."

I am learning not to over-inflate praise. We do it with every good intention to motivate a little learner. But when they don't do something that is wow-worthy, our reaction can be loud – even when we don't voice it out. They notice that, this time round, instead of saying: "Oh wow! Absolutely brilliant! Who's a clever girl?" we say, "That's good. Just keep trying." Their confidence is pierced.

I am learning to teach my daughters that being hard working is better than being clever. And I believe it. I can see the progress that they make when we put in a few minutes of something consistently.

I try hard not to compare. Not to compare my daughters with each other. Not to compare them with their cousins. Not to compare them with their peers. And indeed, not to compare them with myself. It is difficult not to make comparisons. But it is also counterproductive to do so. I am learning to watch for what their different strengths are. And trying to create an environment in which learning is about fun and curiosity. Most importantly, when I start feeling the panic creeping in, I force myself to remember that what they need most is to feel loved, valued and appreciated for all the wonderful things that they are. It is difficult. But I wake up every day reminding myself that we can do hard things. I will keep trying. It also helps that my daughters call me out on my inconsistencies. When I tell Mirembe that she should be like Kirabo, who doesn't cry when she gets something wrong, she reminds me: "People are different Maama. We all feel things differently."

As I teach my children about Maths and Geography and English and History, I also teach them about God and Kindness and Chores and Empathy and Physical Fitness. I let them have many pockets of unscheduled time where they come up with their own games, without me trying to pump my carefully curated world views of success into their unpolluted and beautiful minds.

Perspective: I challenge myself to think about the whole picture. It is easy to point out the things that my children are not doing well and forget to acknowledge the many things that they are doing well. My friend Zelah reminded me to "catch them doing good". I need to remember that more often.

It is sometimes difficult for me not to panic. It can be difficult when you notice that your child is bringing home a book from the red book band when their friend is taking home a higher band like blue or green. It can be difficult not to panic when your child read a word so well yesterday, yet they are struggling to pronounce that very same word today. When they aced the column additions yesterday and today, they are looking at it like it is something from an alien world. It can be difficult not to panic when they write "01" instead of "10" and proudly call "eighteen" "eighty".

But when we panic and use statements like: "What's wrong with you? You read this word JUST YESTERDAY! Are you even interested in learning?", we need to be mindful of the impact of these words on our children. Watch them when you say those things. Are they looking at you with proud enthusiasm or are they shrinking in shame? Are their necks elongated with the pride of a giraffe or are they holding their heads in frustration, as if they are about to burst from the realization that the world is such hard place to be in? Are they speaking confidently, or do they begin to stammer?

I realized that, without intending it, I was slowly – sometimes even quickly – chipping away at the confidence of my otherwise happy and confident little girls. I have had to remind myself on multiple occasions that I am not a lawyer and a neurosurgeon and a Geography teacher and an engineer and an artist and an award-winning movie director and a chef and an actuary. Why would I expect my children to be all these things?

I also realize that I will fall into a panic every now and then. I will tell myself that I will not. But I will. Because I have been so programmed to compare, it is taking me a long time to get unprogrammed. Because there are test scores and report cards to remind me of where on the ladder my children are standing, it is hard not to try to climb those ladders. Because I am human.

My job is to remind myself that panic does not build. It crumbles. And when I do panic and make mistakes, as I will every now and then, I need to forgive myself and then ask my children for forgiveness. And I need to mean it when I say, "I am really sorry. I should not have said that. I will do better next time." And then try and do better next time.

I realize that some of my triggers are rooted in my childhood. The belief that my worth was tied to my academic intelligence. The reminder from my cousin that I would need to compensate for my lack of beauty with academic qualifications. Even though I have grown a whole lot over the years, there is probably still a segment of my sub conscience that puts a premium on academic astuteness. It did, after all, in many ways, save me.

But there is something else. Another kind of fear. A fear that is rooted in my Blackness. Indeed, perhaps, our collective (African) Blackness. There is a reason why Black people, particularly African immigrants, are obsessed with grades and a formal education. There is a reason why we panic when our children tell us that they want to become musicians or gymnasts or artists or footballers. We can entertain these aspirations as long as our children understand that they are just "sides" – not their career goals. We feel threatened when our children treat them

like serious career paths. It is a fear that is deeply rooted
in history. A history in which colonial rule rewarded
formal schooling by elevating it above traditional ways
of knowing. Where those who obtained a British education were promoted above the chiefs and elders who
possessed local knowledge. It explains why, even today,
we assume that a person who speaks English is more
intelligent than a person who speaks Luganda or Lugbara.
It is the reason why we circulate videos on social media
that mock a person who speaks "broken" English. It is
the reason why we believe that a person who wears a suit
is more civilized than a person who wears a *gomesi*. Our
lived experiences teach us that we are more likely to be
granted a visa to visit or live in Canada or the United
Kingdom or United States when we produce a degree
certificate and a letter from our corporate employer than
when we say that we run a business or are a member of
a music band. Our visas are more likely to be renewed
when we have professional jobs as lawyers or doctors or
accountants than when we are aspiring artists or self-em-
ployed entrepreneurs.

Education means something different to us as Black
immigrants. It is often the ticket which allows us to remain
in our host countries. However, since these countries are
sometimes also the home countries of our children, we
oscillate between two worlds. A world where we tem-
porarily entertain the possibility that our children can
dare to follow their dreams on the one hand and a world
where the reality of visa extensions and renewals reminds
us that those dreams are too costly and that it is reckless

to dare to pursue them. When I hear my well-meaning white friends talk about how they don't want to push their children, how their children just need to play, how a certain regime seems too strict and thus unpleasant, I have to climb over a whole pile of trauma to believe that my children can enjoy the same luxuries.

Dear Maama.
It is Well.

Dear Maama
I did it.
Again.

I yelled
And it feels terrible.

I have told myself
Again and again
That I will exercise more patience
Next time.
Next time
I will be more calm
Remembering
That they are children
Being children.

Do you also yell, fellow maama?
Does it make you feel like a terrible mother?

Unable to command her emotions?
Impulsive?
Inadequate?
Guilty?
Incompetent?
Impatient and
Bad?

I gave them ice lollies, fellow maama.
Despite the fact that
It was freezing outside
Their noses
Bloated with colds.

The day before?
We binged on
Chocolate chip cookies
Potato crisps
Culminating with a frozen dinner.
I did feel guilty afterwards.
But in that moment
It felt so good
They were so happy
And I was too tired.
It is well.

Do you sometimes worry, fellow maama?
About the milestones?
Baby not crawling (yet)?
Toddler not speaking (yet)?

Three years old
Still in nappies?
Not sleeping through the night?
Do you worry
That they cannot pronounce
A to Z?
Like their little friend
Next door?
It is well
Fellow maama.

You know those pictures?
Of sweet little girls and boys?
Laughing and smiling?
Like perfect little humans?
Nothing like the little people
In front of you right now?
Well, I have those pictures too, fellow maama.
Plenty pretty.
Sometimes, I take them right before a toddler meltdown.
Other times
Moments after my impulsive yelling.
It's not that I am lying about my life
When I post them on social media.
It's just much easier
Communicating pretty moments.
Remember that, fellow maama,
When your household and your little ones
Look nowhere as cute as mine.

You see, fellow maama
It is a tough job being a mum.
It's tough
When other mums seem like they were born into it.
It's tough
When your husband wonders out loudly
How his own mother did it
When she had plenty more children.
It's tough.
Which is why, fellow maama
You need to give yourself a break.
Let them create a mess
Let them cry some
Eat some junk.
Reach their milestones
In their own time.
Let them
Be children.

Meanwhile
You?
You need to take care of you.
Without guilt.
Put your feet off the ground
Every so often.
Stop.
Do nothing.
And when you yell
As you sure will sometimes
Forgive yourself.

Say sorry.
Maybe next time you will do better.
Maybe you will be more patient.
Or maybe not.

Still
It is well.

MARJORIE JULIAN

I CANNOT TALK ABOUT motherhood without talking
about Marjorie (Marj) Julian.

I met Marj and Jack Julian through my Ghanaian sister-friend, Amma, when I had just completed my Master's
degree. I had submitted my thesis before the end of the
summer but wanted to stick around Kingston, Ontario
until the fall so that I could attend the graduation ceremony. There was one problem. I had run out of money
and could not afford to pay rent for the two months
before graduation. Because I was an international student, who was no longer enrolled at a university, I was
not eligible to work.

As luck would have it, my other Ugandan sister-friend,
Sophia, was just about to start the same programme that
I had completed. Sophia kindly offered to accommodate
me for the two months before graduation. However, it
turned out to be extremely difficult – if not impossible
– to find a homeowner who would allow the two of us
to rent one room.

Luckily (or so we thought), we finally found a place that was being sublet by another university student who was living with his wife. He was also an international student, but he had lived in Kingston much longer than us. The conditions of our tenancy turned out to be quite dodgy. First, there was another set of tenants (a husband and wife – also international students) that were staying in the living room. We had not been informed about them. We only found out when we were moving in our first set of belongings. Then, our new "landlord" insisted that we could not bring any guests into the apartment. All our visitors would have to meet us at the McDonald's across the street. We didn't sign any formal contract (which was odd, given that both Sophia and I are lawyers. But I have also learnt that being in a precarious position has a way of robbing you of your confidence and quickly sucking you into a tunnel of smallness). Our new landlord simply acknowledged on a small piece of paper that he had "received $790 from Sophia XXX".

It quickly became clear to us that this was going to be a complicated arrangement. But since we did not really have many options (other than me leaving town so that Sophia could find more suitable accommodation), we decided that we would stick it out for the two months. After this, Sophia would find a new place.

Amma was renting a room in Marj and Jack's house. For the first couple of weeks since arriving in Kingston, Sophia stayed with Amma. It's a long story, given that Sophia and Amma were not known to each other before then. The short version of the story is that my landlady went back on her promise to let Sophia stay with me for the two weeks, telling me on the day before Sophia's flight was scheduled to arrive that Sophia would have to pay rent for the two weeks. I didn't bother Sophia with this new development. Instead, my Ghanaian sister-friend, Elsie, and I spent the whole evening on our phones, reaching out to friends, trying desperately to find a place for Sophia to stay. Amma spoke to Marj and Jack, who allowed Sophia to lodge with Amma in her room.

On the day that Sophia and I were supposed to move the rest of our belongings into our new dodgy apartment, Marj and Jack casually asked us about the place. We told them – also casually – about the conditions that had been imposed on us. We added that as soon as I left, Sophia would find another place.

The following conversation ensued:

Marj: You cannot live in that apartment. You can't move in with such appalling conditions.

Sophia: I will move out as soon as Jalia leaves Kingston. Right now, this is the only place that we have been able to find, which accepts the two of us to stay in one room for the price of one person's rent. We have already paid the rent. And anyway, I can't afford to pay rent at another place until I get funding later this month.

Marj: The most important thing right now is that you [Sophia] get a good place to stay because you are going to be here for the longer term. I will lend you money for rent. You can pay it back when you get your funding.

Sophia: But what about Jalia?

Marj: Jalia can stay here with us in the spare room.

JALIA KANGAVE

Big fat tears started rolling down our cheeks – Sophia, Elsie (who, bless her, had stuck with us throughout the drama and was as disturbed as we were) and I. We looked at this gentle, soft-spoken, elderly white woman, who had met these three young Black women for the first time only a couple of weeks earlier, offering not just to lend Sophia money, but also to house me, for free, for two whole months.

Her reasoning? She hoped that if her daughter was in a similar position, someone would do the same thing for her. How she could trust Sophia, who she barely knew, with all that money? "If you are a friend of Amma's, I know that I can trust you."

The room that I would occupy for the next two months was a room that Marj and Jack sometimes let out to university students, who would be arriving around the same time that I was moving in.

I stayed with Marj and Jack for two wonderful months. They fed me and made time for me. On graduation day, even though my biological parents were not around to witness the ceremony, I had a new set of parents who, along with Sophia, and Elsie's husband, proudly cheered when our names were called out. In the evening, Marj organized an intimate dinner for me at home: steak, mashed potatoes and sautéed vegetables. We had pumpkin pie for dessert.

When I say that I have been immensely blessed, I am talking about the blessings of people like Marj. People who look at a young woman who looks nothing like them and say, "If my daughter was in your position, I would hope someone would do the same for her." People who look at me and see their daughter. Despite the differences in our skin pigmentation.

IDENTITY AND RACE

M Y HUSBAND AND I had made the decision, long before I conceived our first daughter, that our children would bear Kiganda names. As soon as we found out that it was going to be a girl, we started combing through books, searching on the internet and consulting with knowledgeable individuals about names and the meanings of names. We saw this not just as the birth of a child but, naively, also as the rebirth of a culture that we felt was slowly but steadily being eroded. In fact, I secretly fantasized about that magical moment when we would reveal the name to our family and friends. I pictured them being in awe of us and thinking: *hhhhhhmmmmm, I wonder why we didn't think of this wonderful idea before!* We knew of some people who had made the decision to give their children only native names. But these were very much in the minority. Most of the people that we knew had a combination of a native name and a foreign name (which is often referred to as the religious name).

My fantasies turned out to be misplaced.

Shortly after we announced the names, chaos erupted. Our parents, in particular, were not happy with the decision and strongly contested it. Our initial excitement of wanting to be authentically and proudly Ugandan was quickly punctured. We were immediately bombarded with questions: *What were we thinking? Why did we want to be different? What kind of Muslims were we when we refused to give our child an "Islamic name"? Why did we want to bring shame and heartache to the family? How would our parents explain the absence of an "Islamic name" to the rest of our relatives? What would people in the community think of them? Why this abomination?*

It did not cool their nerves when we explained that we had every intention of raising our children as Muslims. It did not matter when we reminded our parents that the names Mariam and Muhammad and Fatimah and Musa were Arabic names, not Muslim names; and that, in fact, there were many people in Arabic-speaking countries who were called by those names but who were not Muslims. We added that what made someone a Muslim was proclaiming their belief in one God and accepting that the Prophet Muhammad (peace and blessings of Allah be upon him) is Allah's messenger.

None of these explanations eased their fears. What mattered to them was that we had to also be seen to be Muslim. And one litmus test for that was the choice of Arabic names.

Even though in the weeks, months and even the years that would follow, I often found myself frustrated and disheartened by our parents' attitude, deep down I knew that this was not about us loving our culture more than our parents loved it. Rather, it had to do more with how much our parents loved us and what they perceived to be best for us and their grandchild. To understand where they were coming from, context and history are important.

Historically, our ways of knowing and being had been castigated by colonizers as being primitive and backward. Consequently, our culture and beliefs were replaced with other people's ways of knowing and being. The civilizing mission, it was called. And so, when I went to secondary school, there was the one-inch rule. It was an all-girls' school. We were all required to keep our hair one inch long (or short, for that matter). Well, all of us Black girls. The rule did not apply to mixed-race girls and girls of other races, who could keep their hair as long as they wanted it. The school administration's official line was that short hair was much easier to manage. We were not given the option of deciding whether or not we could manage our hair.

What did that say to us as Black girls? Well, first, that our natural hair was unruly. It needed to be tamed. Second, that our hair was unsightly. It needed to be chopped off. And third, that girls of other races had better hair – which meant that our hair was less than (and perhaps, then, that we were also less than). And so we grew up not being proud of our hair. It is little wonder then that, as soon as we finished secondary school, the first thing most of us did was to perm our hair (using chemicals that often burnt our scalps) or wear synthetic hair extensions (most of us could not afford the natural hair extensions).

While the one-inch rule made us ashamed of our natural hair, the rule against speaking native languages made us look down on our culture and our origins. There was a strict rule against speaking "vernacular" on the school grounds. The punishment when you were caught was to wear a sack – a filthy sisal bag that had been used to store dry foods such as beans and maize flour. The sacks had been cut in the shape of a dress, but they remained unsightly. It was the last thing that a self-respecting teenage girl wanted to be caught wearing.

Anyone caught speaking Luganda or Lugbara or Lusoga or Runyankore or any other of the many native languages of Uganda would be given the sack. The responsibility of passing on the sacks was on the people wearing them. With the exception of a few naughty girls, most of us avoided the sack like the plague. For many of us, the sack was a symbol of shame, not just because of how it looked and smelled, but also because of what it represented. Native languages were perceived to be inferior. Girls who spoke native languages were thought of as being backward; or the commonly used word "local" (that is, not modern). There was, however, no punishment for speaking German or French or Arabic. Needless to say, there was no punishment for speaking English.

I did not wear a sack even once for all the four years that I attended the school. I had grown up not speaking much Luganda and was not ashamed of my bankruptcy in that regard. If anything, I felt "cool" and polished when fellow students told me that I had an *akso* (slang for accent). That was a huge compliment. To have an *akso* meant that I sounded foreign, which also meant that I sounded modern and well-travelled. In other words, I was not "local".

How then, did I become the woman who was fighting to give her children Kiganda names? How did I move from being the girl and young woman who was proud of not speaking my native language to being the woman who almost fell out with her parents because of insisting that her children would bear Kiganda names? Was it, as some suggested, me letting a man (my husband) brainwash me and dictate the path that we should take? Had the Permanent Head Damage (PhD) got to my head?

Well, incidentally, it had something to do with education. While I had gone to Canada with the hope of coming back not just more educated, but perhaps also more "white" (i.e. with a more pronounced *akso*, dressing and behaving foreign), my education in Canada turned out to be a pilgrimage to my Blackness. There was something about the Master's programme and later, the PhD, which changed the trajectory of how I thought about myself and about my origin. Canada, being a country with a troubled history of indigenous people, was fertile ground in which to sow the seeds of cultural pride.

The Baganda have a saying – *okutambula kwekumanya* (to travel is to learn). My classes in legal theory would soon expose me to a history of racism and "otherness" that had been erased from the colonial curriculum that Uganda had inherited from Britain. There, I would struggle with the painful realization that the knowledge of my people had been appropriated and misappropriated.

That my people's ways of knowing and being had been undermined and often erased in the name of the civilizing mission. And, even worse, that I had been anointed into this civilizing mission by being made to believe that my history was irrelevant, my language was inferior and my culture was backward.

Yet my real education often happened outside the classroom. My real education happened when, during talent shows, I had nothing authentic to showcase. Was I an African American to lay claim to hip-hop? Which of our traditional dances could I comfortably perform? What did I know about our drums and our folklore? How eloquently could I speak and think in Luganda? My real education came from seeing how Canadian-born graduate students of Chinese origin would bring their parents to Vancouver to teach their infants and toddlers Mandarin and other aspects of Chinese culture. My real education came from witnessing the pride and confidence with which my sister-friends Ibironke and Mosope pronounced and carried their Yoruba names. It came in observing how my sister-friend, Shiva, not only spoke fluent Farsi, but also frequently attended gatherings with fellow Iranians in which they bathed themselves in rich Iranian poetry while munching on crunchy pistachios and nibbling on succulent dates.

I knew then, without a doubt, that I would need first to be un-educated and then re-educated. I needed to be un-educated to get rid of the poison that had been injected in me for decades. The one which made me look down on the ways of my people. The one which made me think that white people were superior because of the colour of their skin, the straightness of their hair and the language that formed in their mouths when they spoke. The one that made me think that my culture was primitive and backward.

I needed to be re-educated in the ways of my people. In the healing properties of our herbal medicines. In the deliciousness of our language and the colourfulness of our spirit. I needed to embrace the wisdom behind our sense of community and the richness of our collective spirit.

When our little girl was born, it was important that she had a name that reminded her of her origin.

Education can buy you certain things as a Black person. With an education, you can afford a ticket to watch the opera or reserve a table at an expensive restaurant. Your academic qualifications can help with visa applications and get you a house in high-end "white" neighbourhoods. Your education can get you invited to prestigious conferences and give you a chair on boards of big companies and international not-for-profit organizations. But education does not guarantee that you will be included or accepted. It does not guarantee that you will be seen or heard. It does not protect you from the reality of your Blackness. Even though we no longer have "Black" and "White" inscriptions on toilet doors or bus seats, there are other ways in which Black people are reminded of the thick lines that separate Blackness from whiteness.

In December 2019, my sister, my daughters, my nieces and I went to watch the Cinderella pantomime in

London, United Kingdom. My sister had secured us great front row seats, which promised to deliver a memorable experience for the children. However, because we were running late, we got there a few minutes into the show and so the ushers asked us to sit at the back until the interval. This was a reasonable request: we did not want to disrupt anyone. And so, we quickly and silently went to the back. During the break, we went to look for our seats. There, we found a white lady with her two children and a man who appeared to be her father. We told the lady that we had come to take up our seats. She looked at us with surprise plastered on her face and said that we must be mistaken – those were their seats. I looked at our tickets again, just to make sure that we were in the right place. I was not mistaken. We were in the right place. She asked to have a look at our tickets. I showed them to her. Looking shocked, she said

"This must be a mistake! We have the same seat numbers!"

I did not ask to look at their tickets. I didn't want to seem confrontational. As Black women, we have been socialised to try as much as possible not to appear angry. Our anger makes (white) people uncomfortable. It is interpreted as uncouth. It is scary. It cannot be tolerated. My sister and two of my nieces had gone to get drinks. As my daughters and my other niece awkwardly stood there, towering over this delicate white woman who now seemed helpless, her children distressed and her old father seeming more frail, I could sense the accusation and suspicion in the eyes of the spectators.

Silence has a loud voice.

As my daughters, my nieces and I stood there in all our Blackness – with our big afros and our colourful clothes – the eyes that poked into us seemed to be asking: "Are you really sure that you have the right seats?" "Do you really belong here and not there (at the back)?"

I asked my niece to stay with her cousins as I went to get an usher. The usher came just as my sister and other nieces were returning. As I explained to my sister what had happened, the usher asked the lady for their tickets and told her that they were seated in the wrong place. More shock on her face. My sister, tired from years of having to be a cheerful and non-confrontational Black woman, and realizing that the lady was still not budging, went and whispered something in her ear. The lady's face turned red. To this day, I have never asked my sister what she said. But it got the lady to stand up, her face almost bleeding from whatever emotion she was feeling.

After the lady and her family moved, an old white lady who had been watching all along leaned forward and said to us:

"She knew that she was lying all along. When you went to get the usher, her father asked her to see their tickets and he told her 'But these are not our seats!' She just kept quiet." The old lady advised: "You should ask the theatre for compensation."

We didn't ask for compensation. What would have been a lot more rewarding than any compensation would have been having even just one person standing up for us. Just one person seeing us. Just one person – maybe the old lady – saying "Hey, I heard that. Will you please move away so that this lovely family can take their seats?"

And yet I also question whether I would have acted differently had I been in the spectators' shoes. It requires a certain amount of courage to speak up and stand out. A courage that is in rare circulation. A courage that is not possessed by many of us. Including me.

Just like I never thought of myself as a feminist, I didn't consciously think of my Blackness until I had several encounters with racist "slights". It happens the first time and you dismiss it as an oversight. It happens again and you make another excuse: maybe it is just a mistake. And then it happens again and you begin to wonder whether it is really just another oversight. Another mistake. These incidents do not necessarily happen with the same people or within the same organization. But when they keep happening to the same person, to you, they become one too many.

It is amazing how, as Black people, our faces can be perceived as threatening on the one hand and yet also be unseen on the other hand. How our bodies can be threatening to a fragile white body in one scenario and yet totally disappear in another scenario. I have been unseen on a number of occasions. A committee on which I volunteer is allocated tasks and everyone, except me, gets a task, despite the fact that I put my hand up. A workshop is organized around a paper that I co-authored and the organizers forget to include my name among the presenters, even though I indicated my eagerness and availability to present. A bubbly polling station official eagerly greets and chats with each of the seven or eight voters who are ahead of me in the queue. But when it comes to my turn, he is magically rendered mute. He looks away, avoiding my glance every time I try to say hello. I hear his bubbly voice come back to life again when I step into the station. He is speaking to the person who was right behind me. He is chatting away to the other voters when I walk out after casting my vote.

We call them "slights". But they have significant consequences. When we are unseen in this manner, we are dehumanised. When we are unseen in our work, we are not just denied the opportunity to be heard but we are also denied opportunities for growth.

It is exhausting to have to remind people that you exist. Why should we have to ask? Why should we be the ones to remind people that we exist when they conveniently remember us when it suits them? Why should we be made to look like the troublemakers? The party poopers? The angry ones?

It gets exhausting. You fight some battles and you let others slip away. Not because they do not matter but because you do not want to subject yourself to the pain that results from someone claiming that they did not realize what they were doing. Or worse still, denying your claims.

These encounters with racism – conscious or unconscious – never leave you quite the same. Before you know it, your generous and cheerful smile is replaced with an official "good morning" or "good afternoon". You give up trying to prove to people that you are, actually, quite amiable. You stop hanging around for small talk and opt for quick hellos and equally quick goodbyes. You stop volunteering to sit on committees. You become less attached, reminding yourself that this is not your home. These are not your people. You agonize over the conversations that you may need to have with your six – and seven-year-old daughters to prepare them for what might happen. A name that they may be called. A false history that they may be taught. A playground game gone wrong, which may result in them being told to "go back to where you belong". And so, you armour up.

You do not do all this because you stop loving people, nor because you stop treasuring a sense of community, but because you realize that your heart is so tender that you don't trust its capacity to hold any more pain. It cannot handle any more rejection. It cannot handle any more exclusion. It cannot handle any more excuses. You choose instead to surround yourself with the allies that you have come to trust over time. The people who see you. The ones who also choose you. The colleague who uses their privilege to speak up against exclusion and fights for your seat at the table. The mum at your children's school who is not afraid to have uncomfortable conversations about racism. The women in your nest who do not have to talk about race, but who you know without a doubt will stand up and speak up when they sense any element of discrimination. These are your people.

Dealing with Grief

By Annette Tush

Any kind of writing is tough. But writing this particular chapter has been incredibly difficult. Death is so surreal, so numbing that such a write-up awakens all the fears still echoing and un-numbs the pain still lingering in the deepest hemispheres of the cerebellum. There is an immeasurable pain that comes with losing a loved one. It brings us to our knees and makes us helpless. It hurts. It hurts recounting circumstances that surrounded the death for it forces you to interact very intimately with painful feelings that have been shelved. It hurts imagining the milestones you would have achieved together. It hurts that you will never see them again. It just hurts.

And how do I know this? Well, I have had my share of losses over the years. In November 2006, I lost my only one and beloved daughter, Ttendo Audrey, just after her first birthday. In 2018, my baby brother, the one that followed me, tragically died. He was barely 30 years old. Shortly after that, my big sister, our firstborn, the pillar of our home, died. And in 2019, I lost my father. And all of this is without counting the dear friends that I have lost, whose deaths have also hurt terribly. Grieving is painful and that pain really never goes away. There is a void that is never filled. Grief can also be super lonely. A loneliness that often leads us to those dark places where everything seems to lose meaning, and life seems to have no purpose. The food we enjoyed, the hobbies we delighted in, the places we loved, the scents we adored. Everything becomes meaningless.

Obviously, each death is different, and the magnitude of the pain felt can only be explained by the person experiencing it. Although I have had many losses, the focus here will be Ttendo's life, how it ended prematurely, the roller coaster I went through following her passing and some healthy ways I have employed to come to terms with this heart-wrenching loss.

Ttendo's Life

IT WAS A FEW minutes past midnight in October 2005 when our little Ttendo was born via c-section, barely ten months after our wedding. Having been in labour for close to two days with no progress, I had to be rushed to the theatre to save our lives. We were both in distress. About six hours later, after I regained consciousness from the anaesthetic drugs that had intoxicated me, I opened my eyes to this beautiful doll. Audrey Ttendo Arinaitwe. I held her in my arms. Our eyes locked. I fell in love. Except for being frail and tired, she was perfect in every way. Here I was – a mother. Ttendo's mother. My husband and I were more than ready for Ttendo: we were ecstatic. We were discharged from the hospital about two days later. Ttendo completed our lives. She was beautiful in every way. We enjoyed parenthood, together. Life was beautiful.

All mothers think that their kids are cute but Ttendo was exceptionally beautiful. I remember fielding several questions about whether I was her mother because most people did not see the resemblance. Those who have used public transport in Kampala, Uganda, understand how nosey and rude those idle people in the taxi park can be. Even though their comments used to get on my nerves, a part of me understood where their rude remarks came from. Ttendo was her dad's duplicate, very light-skinned, long cheekbones and a long well curved forehead (all considered beauty traits by Ugandan standards). I had big plans, mother-daughter plans. I especially wanted to raise her as a strong bold woman who knew her worth, a woman who would never settle for less when it came to men. Oh, how I had plans!

Unfortunately, those plans never materialized. At about six months of age, Ttendo started getting unexplained seizures. Whether that prolonged labour caused asphyxia that led to those seizures, whether they were genetic or as a result of witchcraft like some suggested, we will never know. To this day, we have no answers. We sought medical advice from hospitals. We visited renowned traditional healers. We gave her medicine and administered herbs. We took her to church for prayers. We did what we could to make Ttendo feel better. But the seizures just intensified. Six months later, she succumbed to one strong seizure that lasted for close to twelve hours.

The morning following that painful seizure attack, we took Ttendo to her usual doctor, who did a brief assessment and sent us back home. We didn't get home because she seemed to be getting worse. We immediately made a U-turn and headed to Mulago Hospital, the main referral hospital in Uganda. Luckily, I was with my sister-in-law who was a nurse at the hospital. Once we got admitted, things happened at lightning speed. My sister-in-law changed into her scrubs, hunted down all the doctors she could find, hooked little Ttendo on some intravenous rehydration tubes and doctors and nurses surrounded the bed with stethoscopes, hovering over her frail body. Ttendo died about two hours after we got to the hospital. I realized that all along, she had been in a coma fighting for her life. How the first doctor failed to detect that will always remain a mystery to me.

I hugged and embraced Ttendo's warm body, thinking she would hug me back, but she remained still. I kept hoping that it was another seizure and that she would eventually wake up, but I was wrong. Her frail body just lay there. It is hard to explain that feeling. I was helpless. I did not know what to do. My brain froze. A few hours later, I found myself being led to the car that would take her home from the hospital. We headed back to Gayaza High School where I was teaching and living the time. The school was in a sombre mood. The girls and the staff wailed like little babies when we entered the main gate. It began to sink in. Ttendo was gone.

Even with her seizures, it never crossed my mind that Ttendo would die at such a tender age. I thought she was going to outgrow them. I had been told stories of several people who had seizures and lived fruitful lives. Why not my daughter? It was bizarre. Even today, Ttendo's death still remains the most inexplicable moment I have ever experienced and will probably remain so for life.

Why Ttendo's Death Was Heart-Wrenching

NOT ALL DEATHS ARE the same. There are unique circumstances associated with each death that make each encounter particularly painful. It could be the special bond one had with the deceased; a sudden death that gives the loved ones no chance for final goodbyes; unusual circumstances like coronavirus or Ebola that keep families in quarantine, denying them an opportunity to grieve together; the role the person played in one's life (financial, moral support); gossip about how the death could have been prevented; lack of finances to deal with funeral expenses; the hopes that one had in the deceased person; and so on. Ttendo's death had components of most of these.

For starters, Ttendo was our only child at that time. My firstborn. The apple of my eye. Losing your only child can be emotionally disconcerting. Her death left me feeling empty, alone, and deserted. For the little time she had lived, Ttendo had become my little friend, my joy, and my life revolved around hers. We even shared a bed. I rationalized that if I had other children, it would have been easier to deal with the pain since I would still have children to focus my energy on. Now, in hindsight, I see how difficult it can be to grieve with other children in the picture. Moreover, regardless of how many children one has, each child is unique, and nothing lessens the pain of losing one of them. In that moment however, my mind was consumed with "what if" questions. "What if I was unable to conceive another child? What if, just like Ttendo, all my children never lived beyond one year? What if… what if?" So many what ifs, but very few answers. That was scary.

Secondly, my husband was away. It had been about two months since he had left to pursue further studies in Canada, leaving us (my Ttendo and I) in Uganda. The plan had been for him to go, complete his course and come back to us. How was I to break such news to him, that his daughter, his duplicate, daddy's daughter was no more? Perhaps more terrifying was the fact that I had to deal with this alone. Having been married for only two years, we completely relied on each other. It was just a year before when he had camped on the labour ward floor waiting to receive his daughter. Unlike most traditional men who leave women to raise children, he is different. He had (and has always) been there, very actively involved. We had been raising her together. How was I to deal with this all alone? And how was he to grieve alone across the oceans with no family around him? It broke my heart. I felt his pain.

Then, there were the self-appointed judges who seemed to love Ttendo more than we did, and somehow knew what we should have done to prevent her death. They talked and they talked and they talked some more. And these were not strangers. Some were people from our inner circles, those I trusted the most and called friends. I was blamed and condemned for what I did or did not do to save our daughter. Knowing that the people we trusted the most, people who knew Ttendos's story, people who knew how the past six months or so had been for us, were talking behind our backs pierced through my heart like a dagger.

Because of everything that was going on, I ceased being myself. I felt a sense of guilt and shame, as if I had caused my daughter's death. Why didn't I look for more experienced doctors? Why didn't I give the other medicine instead? Why did I delay going to the referral hospital? The questions rippled in my mind. All I wanted to do was to coil in bed all day long. I didn't want to be part of the world. I stayed away from social gatherings. I blamed the doctor who had treated her shortly before she passed on. I kept thinking: had she been keener and more diligent, she would have immediately referred us to the hospital and maybe those hours we wasted moving back and forth could have saved her life. I rationalized. I felt so angry. I blamed God. I cursed Him. I asked questions (and I still do). I developed anger and hatred for those that had uttered piercing comments. I confronted others. I felt a sense of betrayal. I started feeling uncomfortable around babies. I started imagining that if I ever had other children, they would never grow past their first birthday. Indeed, when we later had our son, going past the age of one became very traumatizing. I would often wake up in the middle of the night, sweating profusely as if he was going to die. A simple cold would throw me into panic. My life was becoming a mess. A total mess... but then things started turning around.

Today, while I get those intermittent episodes, I am in a much better place than I was years ago. Obviously, some days are more difficult than others. Days such as these when I am compelled to recount events that took her from me; days like her birthday when I keep wondering what kind of girl she would have become and the milestones she would have achieved; days when her brothers keep lamenting how they wish they had a sister; days when I feel outnumbered as one lady among four men; days when I go shopping and wish I had someone to do silly stuff with. I especially detest days when I see a mother lose her child. It brings back those fresh memories. Yes, some days are just difficult, but I have come a long way. I will share, in no particular order, the things that have helped and are still helping me (us) not just rise but also shine despite the great loss we have suffered.

My General Approach to Life and Faith in God

MY PERSONALITY IS ONE of my greatest strengths, even though it can occasionally be catastrophic. I am a very passionate person who gives my all to whatever comes my way: relationships, work, education, parenting and so on. I go all the way in. When things take a different turn, it is usually relatively easy for me to move on, knowing that I did all I could. As I grow older, I also keep confirming that crying over spilt milk doesn't really change much. Rather, it is best to learn from that experience and move on. And that was pretty much how I dealt with Ttendo's death.

Whether it was because Ttendo was our first born or a premonition on my part that she wouldn't be with us for long, I did for her what I presume every mother would do for their first child and some more. For instance, her first birthday celebration was very carefully planned. We made merry and boy, oh boy, that little girl danced and ate cake! On her christening, we went to the village and threw a grand party. She danced and entertained everyone, like she would never get another chance. People equated this celebration to a traditional give away ceremony, where daughters are handed over to their future husbands in marriage. Little did we know that that was going to be her last celebration.

After the initial phase of heightened emotions, I began affirming to myself that I loved my daughter more than everyone else. Also, I convinced myself that, given what I knew at the time, I did the best I could. From seeking

medical help to being there for her as her mother, I felt I had not held back anything. Is there anything I could have done differently? Absolutely! However, I told myself that I did what I could under the circumstances. And that greatly helped.

One of the questions I have failed to answer over the years is why she was taken from us at such a tender age. I have oftentimes wondered if it happened in part to enable me provide comfort to those grieving from similar experiences. And here is why. Before Ttendo died, when I would tell people that somehow, they had to find ways to move on, the common response I always got was "What do you know? You have never lost someone. You do not know what it feels like." Yup, I would be at a loss for words. Now that I had suffered great loss, I had become part of the family of those who had experienced this kind of grief. While experiences are different, there is that common feeling shared by those who have lost their dear ones. Now I can speak to grieving mothers from a lived experience. I can speak to those who have lost their dads. I can speak to those who have lost their siblings. Ttendo's death was particularly life changing for my husband, at least from my perspective. Shortly before we got married, my husband's sister was murdered under dubious circumstances. That death hit him so hard! He blamed himself because he thought he could have prevented it. That experience led him to a very dark place. Every time I tried to talk about it and how it was unhealthy for him to continue on that dark path he was treading, the response was always the same: "What do you know?" After Ttendo's death, and seeing how I dealt with it, I believe it helped my husband realize that you can actually "move on". And that has helped us both.

Ttendo's death confirmed to me that when it comes to death, there is so much that is out of our control, that we just need to surrender. And as my co-author and sister-friend, Jalia, once wrote in one of her musings on social media, surrender "doesn't mean you have lost hope. It doesn't mean you stop praying... it doesn't mean you stop feeling the pain. It means you lean into something bigger than yourself. It means that you acknowledge that there are things beyond your control or understanding. It means that you exercise kindness to yourself by stopping to punish yourself over what you could have done better. It means taking care of yourself (your emotions) in spite of everything that is going on. Trusting that, at the end of the day, God is in control." Surrendering to this supernatural being has been an awesome way for me to cope with Ttendo's death. I am not sure where I would be without God by my side.

Support From Friends and Family

IF THERE IS ANYTHING that has ever overwhelmed me and left an indelible mark on my life, it is the love we received when Ttendo passed away. People's compassion, love and support in every way overwhelmed me. Coping with Ttendo's death could have been extremely difficult if I had to deal with it all alone. Following her death, I blacked out and I was aimlessly gazing into space, helpless and defeated. Within a few minutes of her passing, one of our friends was right there. He knew how bureaucratic Mulago Hospital could be and how releasing the body could cause a lot of stress. He hounded hospital administrators in their offices and moved back and forth on our behalf. Before I knew it, I was being led to the vehicle waiting to take us home, with Ttendo's body in a coffin. I have no idea where that came from and who paid for it. I will not mention names here... but people gave money, travelled long distances for the burial, fasted and prayed for and with us, called and checked on us, and gave us advice (some of it toxic, though with good intentions) and I never felt alone. When we came back from the village after the burial, to my surprise (and disappointment at the time), our place had been cleared of Ttendo's belongings, to shield us from constantly going through her things, thus opening up fresh wounds.

It did not stop there. It was people's love and generosity that enabled me to remain sane when I later lost my sister and brother, both of whom passed away when I was in Canada and unable to go back home for their burials.

These friends embraced us in their love and extended support to my family even in my absence. It was this same support that I received when I lost my father. This experience challenged me to reach out more to those who are grieving. I have been asked why I tend to get too involved when my people lose loved ones and the answer is simple. I do it because I know what that phone call, that extra penny, that word of encouragement, or what just being there means to a grieving heart. If I can remove just one layer of stress from a grieving heart, nothing stops me. I know of people who want to do it all alone but allowing others to carry the pain with you makes grieving a little more bearable. I wish I could do more, but sometimes I don't. Because I am human. But I am forever grateful for my friends and family for without them, I could not have recovered.

My Husband's Support and Vision

THE LAST THING I expected when Ttendo died was my husband coming home for burial. I did not even suggest it to him because I knew the financial hardships. He was barely two months into his graduate programme and coming back did not make much financial sense. To my surprise, he did all he could. He made it for the burial! What a relief! That is the reason I vowed that I would stay married to this dude till death do us part. Being together, mourning together, crying together (though I did the crying), took a huge weight off my shoulders. We did not blame each other. Even when people were passing judgement, we both spoke the same language. Although he had been away, he knew what we had been going through with Ttendo. He had seen her in pain. He knew that in those two months that he was away, I was doing the best I could. If he felt otherwise, at least I did not sense it. And this helped, A LOT. Most couples drift apart because they start blaming each other. And guess what, you can never fail to find something to point to if you choose that path. Choosing the alternative, of supporting one another, goes a long way – it did for us.

Another thing that helped us is that as a couple we have always shared a strong bond. We always share the good and the bad moments together. We have always been a team. While we love our kids, with or without them, our bond can still last – at least that is how I feel. And as one of our friends crudely put it, we knew that "as long as we still had the tools" we would have another child (though random thoughts of doubt often invaded my mind). We were still young and very fertile. Indeed, it did not take long. God worked through one lady in the aftermath. She gathered courage to tell me that if we were able, we should try to have another baby as soon as possible. It sounded weird but we tried. Although many people have different views about this, it worked for us. Our Shawn was born the following year. It did not take the pain away, but it gave me (us) something to look forward to.

But perhaps what helped the most was the ability to make major changes in my (our) life. After the burial, my husband suggested that I go back with him to Canada; just for a few months to recuperate. It was very scary. I was doing well by Ugandan standards and it had never been my desire to go abroad. Leaving my well-paying permanent and pensionable job, leaving my people, and tagging along with my husband in a foreign country where he was just a student, with no regular income, was nerve-racking. But we decided to take that leap of faith. We somehow knew that since we had each other, we would thrive. In January 2007, the plane took off from Entebbe International Airport and landed at Vancouver International Airport, where I almost fainted because of the coldness. What happened after that is history. Those few months became years. Decades later, we are still in North America with three handsome boys.

From this experience, I tell people who are grieving to make changes in their lives, however small. While you might not leave the country like I did, getting something different to occupy your mind goes a long way. It could be a new hobby, a new skill, a more challenging project at work, reading a new book, keeping a journal, taking on more hours at work, etc. You just need to do what you feel you need to do. There is healing in trying out something new. This can be even more therapeutic if what you decide to do is in memory of your loved one. I eventually started the Little Ttendo Foundation, (so that her memory lives on), an organization aimed at helping little girls pay tuition fees so that they get a chance at getting quality education, something that is not guaranteed, particularly for children in rural Africa. That has been rewarding. As a caveat though, it is important to avoid changes that bring fresh memories. For instance, if you lost a child, it might be painful starting a project involving children of the same age, for obvious reasons.

All in all, I count myself lucky that I have such a visionary husband who saw the benefits of making such major changes and made it happen. And of course, I also thank myself for taking that leap of faith.

Final Thoughts

IF THERE IS ONE thing I have learnt through all this, it is the fact that death comes with a blindfold. It makes us believe that no one has ever endured "our" kind of loss, that our experience is isolated and not common. In my case, I considered Ttendo to be the cutest little human being that had ever lived (I still think so), hence no one else knew the magnitude of losing such a cute little pie with a bright future ahead of her. I became self-centred and self-absorbed. Surely no one had ever lost a daughter like mine, right? Wrong! I was dead wrong. While it is true that there was and will never be another Ttendo, what I was going through was a common occurrence. Many families have endured losing their "only" Ttendo. I am not alone. You are not alone. We are not alone.

Following Ttendo's death, many women I had known for years narrated their own painful stories. I had had no reason to suspect that they had suffered such tragic losses because they were full of life and optimism. Some had lost their twins; some had lost the only child they had and had failed to conceive again; others had lost children at different stages, from miscarriages to stillbirths to fully grown self-sufficient adults and still, they were thriving. I remembered that my own sister had had endless mis-carriages, and a stillbirth, yet she was carrying on with life. I thought about my mother-in-law, who had lost her beautiful daughter, the apple of her eye, leaving behind two young babies to raise. My mother-in-law was still living and even thriving. I thought of our neighbour in the village, Nora, who had seven children (five boys and two girls). They were the source of her joy. One by one, I had seen Nora lose her kids, to HIV/AIDS, road accidents and other catastrophes. But Nora was still living and hopeful.

I am not trying to minimize people's experiences because I know your child is your child. Your loss is your loss. And it affects us differently. However, in reality, we are not alone! Accepting this simple truth and learning from other people's experiences makes grieving a bit easier. And now that I see my own mother, carrying on with life, after losing her husband, her daughter, her son and then her grandchildren including my Ttendo, I get the courage to keep moving. I know I am not alone.

Another great lesson I have learnt from all this is that in every situation, however bad, there are things worth being grateful for. Even in death. I have nothing but great memories when I think about my daughter. Ttendo lived her life like a candle in the wind. There was never a dull moment when you were with her. She navigated through life like she knew that her candle would be blown out at any time. Though her flame was blown out prematurely, she left an indelible mark in my life and the lives of those who knew her. Nothing can erase those memories. I beam with joy every time I think about her: her smile which she gave freely, her bear-tight hugs, her swaggerific dance moves and the way she endured pain like a warrior. If you are grieving someone, your task is to find those memories, cherish them and hold them dear to your heart.

Finally, Ttendo's life, together with the lives of those who also departed prematurely, also continues to remind me that our time on Earth is limited and that we should never be complacent. Ttendo died at one, but that girl got out of life what most people (even those who live for decades) might only dream about. She gave all she had without any reservations. That should be a wake-up call for all of us. If your clock stopped ticking today, what would be your biggest regret? Perhaps, now is the time to challenge yourself because when all is said and done, we are all in transition to eternity – the only unknown is when. Live your life with intention for it is just a matter of time until we will be reunited with our loved ones that preceded us. And that means we are bigger than death. When you understand the fact that death really has no power over us, grieving becomes less painful. Today, I strive to do the best I can, so that when my time comes, I will have fulfilled my purpose, just like Ttendo and those who have departed this life before us. That is what I call victory over death.

CAREER AND PURPOSE

MY SOUL SISTER, NURUH, and I used to sit on the top decks of our creaky metallic bunk beds at Nabisunsa Girls' School in the evenings after classes, singing our hearts out and mapping out our dreams. Our favourite song was "Tomorrow", written by the music genius Quincy Jones, and sang by the young, sweet-faced, pure-voiced Tevin Campbell. "If we try, we can fly to a whole 'nother place … We can go anywhere we want, any road we decide to take" we squeaked, accompanying the words with exaggerated actions. The song always breathed fresh and exuberant energy into our youthful zeal and optimism. It strengthened our resolve and belief in our ability to change the world.

The plan was that, once we completed our formal education, Nuruh and I would establish an organization – Children of the World (COTW – pronounced *kotwu*) – which would cater for impoverished children by providing them with opportunities to have an education. It would give them access to the kinds of resources that we were fortunate enough to have because of the relative privilege that we grew up in. Our focus would be street children, who were often shunned in society. We even had a write-up to back our plans. A constitution of sorts.

And then we grew up. And we stopped singing. Nuruh went on to study accounting at university in the United States. I studied law in Uganda. We got "important" jobs. We got married. We started our own families. We existed. Our dreams were relegated to the margins of our busy lives. Work. Children's school projects. Housework. After school activities. Doctor's appointments. More work. A bit of family time. Squeezing in some get togethers with friends. More work.

COTW had been tucked away and indeed, long been forgotten. New dreams emerged. But they also soon took to the back burner. As we went about the everyday business of being adults, we shelved our dreams and concentrated on daily realities. Our ambitions started to get mouldy. Just like the pretty jacket for five-to-six year olds that you buy for your two-year-old daughter, hoping that she will wear it when she turns five. First, you put it on a hanger in the wardrobe. Summer comes. There is not enough space in the wardrobe and so you put it away with the rest of the winter clothing. Because it is still quite big, you put it at the very bottom of the trunk, telling yourself that you will get it when your daughter grows. You forget about it. The next time you look at it, your daughter is eight or ten or fifteen. It does not fit. It is too small. It has even attracted some mould.

Unlike the jacket, however, even when it gathers mould, purpose never completely leaves us. Even when we stash it at the bottom of the pile, it has an unsettling way of reminding us of its presence. About three and a half years ago, Nuruh and I resumed our talks with an urgency and intensity that mirrored our childhood enthusiasm. *Why did God put us on this Earth? Were we really content with our "successful" careers? What were the things that brought us joy when we were younger? What happened to the big dreams that we assembled when we sat on those creaky metallic bunk beds, chewing on roasted peanuts and meketu? How did others manage to pursue their dreams when they had bills to pay?* Our conversations – all held on the phone and each lasting at least two hours – always left us feeling nostalgic and unsettled.

These conversations watered the seed that we had planted almost three decades ago.

In December 2019, I quit my full-time job. I had always known that I would quit full-time employment before I reached retirement age. I had in fact done so before, only to return shortly afterwards, for various reasons (not the least of which was the financial security that a constant pay cheque provides). Still, I did not anticipate that I would walk away again so soon. But in the year preceding my resignation, I had this nagging voice that kept relentlessly pecking at me: *How long do you reckon you can keep this up for? Are you really fulfilled? Is the security of a pay cheque worth the discontent? Are you doing what you came here to do? What other sign do you need? Do you really think it will get easier to walk away next year or the year after or in 2050? Are you showing up in your truest form? When will the "right moment" reveal itself? How will you identify "the sign"?* Another, more rational – and superior sounding – voice would retort: *Who do you think you are? How can you give up a job that many people would give anything to have to pursue something that you are not even clear about? What about all those years that you spent building your career? How do you expect to pay the bills anyway? And what about that mortgage that you have been saving up for? What about the gymnastic classes and the swimming classes and the drama classes for your little ones? Do you think you can pay for those using your blurry dreams? How will you explain your ridiculous decision to your mother and the rest of the clan? What if this doesn't work? Also, please, those are white people problems – white people are the ones with the luxury to agonize over the twin problems of passion and purpose. That self-actualization stuff is not for you. Stay in your lane, Black child. Are you even talented enough?*

Most people write about the risks that they took after they have paid off, financially. Well, I regret to inform you that that is not the case with this writer. Wouldn't it just be script worthy if I told you that I had revived our childhood dream of COTW? That Nuruh and I moved back to Uganda and left behind everything we had built over the years to follow our passion? Well … that has not happened. The truth is, I have no grand plan, let alone a fattened bank account. More than one year later, I am still not sure where I am headed to. I still experience episodes of doubt about my abilities. I stealthily peek into my bank account to make sure that it is still breathing. I sometimes question my sanity when I turn down assignments that would at least ensure some income coming in.

But there is one thing that I am certain about. Even though I do not know where I am going, I have not for one moment questioned my decision to quit my job. I did not question that decision even though 2020, with the coronavirus pandemic, was a scary year and it would have been less scary if I had had a constant pay cheque. Here is the other thing. Despite the fact that I have no grand plans, I am increasingly gaining clarity about the things that I do not want to do. And moving those things out of the picture is creating room for the things that had been buried beneath them. As I unclothe myself of the multiple layers that have served me in the past, but are no longer viable currency, the whisper of *Tomorrow* seems to be drawing closer. After a year of being buried under the fog that was 2020, I feel myself rising to a new dawn and a new song.

Now, when I walk into a meeting, I proudly bring with me the richness of the stories of my people. When I train early career researchers or mentor young people, I am not ashamed to reveal the things that I struggle with. Likewise, when I go into contract negotiations, I am not afraid to turn down an offer that does not reflect my worth. This has not been an easy journey. As a Black Muslim woman, I have often been the recipient of mes-sages (both direct and indirect; subtle and not so subtle), which were intended to remind me of the small corner of life that I should occupy. As a Black person, I grew up in an environment which largely equated whiteness with greatness and Blackness with inferiority. As a woman, I have often been reminded of the superior position that is reserved for men and the sanctity of submitting to manhood. And religious interpretation has promoted wearing modesty as a badge of honour, with a seasoning that is intended to equate modesty with smallness. These three identities that I occupy have often sent various messages. *Do not speak up. Do not question authority. In fact, just don't question. Be modest. Lower your gaze. You can dream – but don't dream so big that you make others uncomfortable. Don't be too ambitious. You will scare men away. Don't talk about your accomplishments. God does not like pride. Don't question white people. They know more. All in all, you were not designed for greatness.* Or simply: shrink.

I recall with slight amusement a hot Sunday afternoon when I stood outside the staffroom at Kibuli Secondary School shouting back at over a dozen teachers who were shouting at me. Kibuli, which I attended for my final two years of secondary school, had some tough regulations around the kinds of clothes that we were expected to wear. We were not allowed to wear short dresses (even though the definition of short was debatable). Also, without explicitly being told so, we knew that it was taboo to question authority. On that dreadful hot Sunday afternoon, my sister and a family friend came to visit me (Sundays were visitation days). My sister was wearing shorts. When she came to the dormitory, the deputy headmaster approached our family friend who had stayed in the car (male visitors were not allowed into female dormitories) and confiscated the car keys from him. The deputy then sent for me. When I got there, the staffroom was on fire. They were talking about the abominable woman who had come dressed in utterly abominable clothing. The teachers started to shout at me. I don't even remember the details of the heated exchange that ensued between about fifteen adult male and female teachers and I, a short and smallish teenage girl. What I do remember is that they were shouting at me and I was shouting back at them. They were pointing fingers at me and I was pointing fingers back at them. I also remember telling them: "You know, I don't like this school. But my parents are not going to take me away from here unless you expel me. So please, do us both a favour and expel me."

Sitting silently in the corner was my history teacher. He was a quiet and principled man. He wore crisply ironed clothes and spoke with a soft but authoritative voice. He was looking at me with both empathy and shock. He had never seen this side of me. I was the obedient student. The one who always sat at the front of the class. The one who always did the homework on class readings that he had assigned to us. The one who contributed to class discussions. The one who was eager to learn. The one who respected my teachers. His face seemed to say to me: *I can see that you have been wronged and provoked. I am sorry I can't speak up for you. But I see you. I hear you.* I was sent back home with my sister that evening.

Some of my friends have called me strong and courageous for the decision that I made to leave full-time employment. I do not necessarily see myself as either of the two. Rather, there is a part of me that could no longer dismiss the rabid pecking of my internal GPS. I was, quite simply, exhausted. I did wait for some kind of rock bottom that would propel me into the pursuit of my purpose. Maybe a misdiagnosis that allowed me just enough time to make the big shift before it was discovered that the doctors were wrong? Or a restructuring that would see me lose my job but walk away with a huge redundancy package that would serve as both a financial cushion and an explanation for leaving a decently paying job for something that I did not know? Well, neither of these things happened.

What happened instead was that I became too exhausted and spiritless, to the extent that I knew that I could no longer continue to do the things that I had been doing. I knew that I needed to stop. I also knew that in my case, this stopping would not involve abrupt shifts that entailed abandoning things altogether in order to soul search. I would not be taking a trip around the world to find myself. My soul searching would not involve climbing Mount Everest in search of answers and inspiration. Neither, for that matter, would it entail totally detaching myself from my previous career in pursuit of new and bold beginnings (even though I flirted with that idea for a while). In my case, I had to live with at least three realities. First, that I was contributing to our household income and needed to continue earning some income so that our livelihood would not come under threat. Second, as a mother of two young girls, I could not just up and leave for a long stretch of time. And third, as an immigrant on a visa without recourse to public funds, I had to ensure that our household income met the minimum financial requirements for me to be able to renew my visa when the time came.

It is, however, also not lost on me that in many ways, I occupy a position of privilege. While as a Black, female, Muslim, immigrant, I belong to a demographic group that has often been marginalized, as an educated, middle class, married woman, with at least some form of documented status, I also belong to a privileged minority. That I can walk away from a secure and decent-paying job is in part testimony to my privileged position. That I can afford to say no to work which does not align with my (unclear) vision is a privilege. That I don't have to worry about my children going hungry or being without a roof over our heads is also a privilege.

For a long time, I felt an awkward need to downplay and/or make excuses for this privilege. To downplay the fact that because my late grandfather had been a wealthy man with a great vision, he had left behind enough wealth to provide some financial cushioning for a single mother that enabled her to lay a strong foundation for the education of her children. Because I was socialised to be modest, I often found myself understating my academic achievements and career milestones because I felt that to disclose them would appear to be boastful. I now know that shrinking myself in this manner – whether to make others feel more comfortable or to make them feel like I am less than them (both of which are normally intended to gain their acceptance and approval) – does not serve me. And it does not serve the people I wish to serve. As Maya Angelou said in one of her classes at the Academy of Achievement in 1990, modesty is quite different from humility.

> I don't think modesty is a very good virtue, if it is a virtue at all. A modest person will drop the modesty in a minute. You see, it is a learned affectation. But humility comes from the inside out. Humility says that there is someone before me, someone found the path, someone made the road before me, and I have the responsibility of making the road for someone who is yet to come.

My hope now is that I grow in humility. That I never forget that my position of privilege is a gift from many great women and men who paved the way for me. Women and men who fought hard for my right to an education, to vote, to work outside the home, to have options. My privilege is not something to be ashamed of. But it creates a responsibility. It is something to use to pave the way for others who will come after me. Young women and men who may have different backgrounds from mine but who want things similar to what I want.

I hope that I can use my life as a class.

Perhaps, then, this is my purpose.

Do You Suffer From
Imposter Syndrome?

W HEN I WATCHED LUPITA Nyong'o's 2014 key-
note address at the Massachusetts Conference
for Women, there were many things that she said that
resonated with me. But it was her definition of imposter
syndrome, "a pattern of toxic thoughts that tells you how
lucky you are to have everybody fooled that you are good
at what you do until ... your cover is blown ..." that
stayed with me. As I listened to her speaking, I kept
thinking to myself: *Oh my God! That is me! I finally have
a diagnosis! I suffer from imposter syndrome!*

I second-guess myself a lot. You know those people
in class who fear to raise their hands because they fear
that their answers are wrong? The people who fear to
speak in meetings because they have this small voice
that keeps telling them that their ideas are ridiculous,
and their questions are silly? And then, as they are still
internally debating about whether and how to say what
they want to say, someone says it? And the teacher or

boss goes: "That's a brilliant idea!" They sit back and kick themselves. They promise to speak up next time. Only to battle with the same demons afresh.

Well, for a very long time, that was me. In fact, in some ways, it is still me.

When I was pursuing my PhD, my supervisor (the intelligent, young and passionate Professor Natasha Affolder), often had to remind me that I needed to trust my voice. She told me that I had brilliant ideas but that I often downplayed them. She said: "Jalia, you are very modest. It's good to be modest. But unfortunately, in this market, when you downplay your achievements and your abilities, people who are less qualified than you will be given the opportunities because they are not afraid to blow their own trumpets." She was right.

But the idea of blowing my own trumpet was quite foreign to me. I had been raised in an environment where modesty was a virtue. Where you did not speak about your achievements because that would be perceived as boastful. You hoped that someone else would speak for you about the things that you were capable of. You waited for your turn to be picked. You prayed that someone would recognize you or magically discover you.

An unintended consequence of modesty is that, because you downplay your achievements, you tend to speak up less and, in turn, you tend to trust your ideas less. In my last job, I was required to take the lead on a number of decisions. Oftentimes, this meant taking some hard decisions and having to own those decisions. I was not accustomed to this kind of autonomy or authority.

I found it scary. And so, naturally, the imposter in me was active. I constantly worried about whether I was making the right decisions. I would think and rethink before responding to an email, including thinking about whether I should respond to the email. I procrastinated. And when I felt overwhelmed, I became mute.

The problem with second-guessing yourself in this manner is that others also begin to second-guess you. Your boss begins to wonder whether they made the right decision in giving you that responsibility. As you are still trying to make up your mind about whether you should or should not do something, others step up and step in. Before you know it, instead of calling on you, your boss and others begin calling on your colleague who is not afraid to take the challenge. If you are an entrepreneur, as you are still trying to figure out whether or not you should start that business in that location, someone else starts up the business in that exact location while you are still waiting for that moment when things will be perfect. When you will be sure. They may be less qualified than you. But because they started with what they had, because they valued growth more than they feared failure, they acted. They are learning along the way. They are doing. You are still waiting for that perfect moment.

To confront the imposter syndrome, I am challenging myself with an "I can" attitude. I am making myself speak up more, even when I am afraid. I am volunteering for more responsibilities so that I increase the opportunities for learning. I am not waiting until it is safe before I put my hand up. This doesn't mean that I simply wish my fear away. It also doesn't mean that I "fake it until I make it". Rather, it means that I speak in spite of my fear.

It also means that I recognize that I have all the ingredients in me to do the things that others do. Sometimes, it may take me a little longer. And there will be times when I do not get it right. But the only way that I can learn is by doing, by showing up, remembering the wise words of Henry Ford: "Whether you think you can, or you think you can't – you're right."

The imposter exists because fear has often stopped me from looking at challenges as opportunities for growth. My default was to opt out of something new to protect myself from the embarrassment of failing. Opting out was always safer. Yet the more I opted out, the fewer opportunities I had to practice. The fewer opportunities I had to learn. The fewer opportunities I had to discover my strengths. I am learning to give up the need to be perfect. The need to have figured out all the answers before I try.

But what happens when, even after denouncing the imposter, fear, uncertainty and self-doubt still creep me? What happens when, even after telling ourselves that we can, we secretly feel that we can't? In other words, what happens when we feel like an imposter every now and then? Does it confirm that we are an imposter?

I tried to completely get rid of the imposter. But I realize that she shows up every now and then – especially when I try to step out of my comfort zone. Instead of letting her talk me into not acting, I am learning to get curious about her. To ask her: *Why is it that you are showing up this time? What are you here to teach me? What is the difference this time round? Oooooh okay. Thank you for your time! Bye bye! I've got this! I will. I can. I too can do hard things.*

IF IT'S DIFFICULT AND CREATES SOME ANXIETY OR FEAR, IT'S PROBABLY WORTH IT

MY DEAR FRIEND, PROFESSOR Ibironke Odumosu (Ronke), once told me when I was whining about a paper that I was writing: "If you are struggling with that paper, it will probably turn out to be a great paper. It's those papers that give you a headache, the ones that you have a hard time piecing together, that often turn out to be some of the best papers you will write." She was speaking from experience. Every time I read something that Ronke has written, I marvel at the beauty of her eloquence. I marvel at how she is able to weave words together so seamlessly, to communicate academic messages so clearly, powerfully and seemingly effortlessly. But I know that it is not without effort. I know the long hours that Ronke puts in. I know that she reads and re-reads and then reads again a paper that she is writing before sending it off for review. The reason her articles read like music to the ears is because she gives them her best and then some. It's often a gruelling process. It sometimes creates anxiety. But because Ronke loves teaching and research, for her, it is totally worth it.

What makes Ronke brilliant at what she does is the fact that she works really hard at it. But that is not a revelation. We all know that, for the most part, successful people are successful because they put a lot of work into what they do. Yet somehow, many of us seem to think that we can wish our way into success. We come up with all kinds of excuses to legitimize why we are not achieving the things that we would like to achieve. "I will pursue my dreams when my kids get older." "I will start writing that book when the kids finish nursery. I will have a lot more time then." "I will start my business when I have fewer bills to pay." "I am too tired or too busy this week. I will start working on that project next week." "If only I did not have a mortgage to pay." "I can't start working on my passion because I have all these other projects that need my attention." "Maybe I should just keep playing the lottery."

I am laughing as I write this because I myself am guilty. I am guilty of frequently making excuses. "I don't know how to do this." "I am too exhausted." "I will start doing research on the book that I want to write next week." I am guilty of feeling sorry for myself because I have young children (which is often a legitimate excuse for not being able to do much).

Here is the thing though. I will always have bills to pay. God willing, I will always have children and as they grow older, they will still need me in different ways. I also have a feeling that days will always have 24 hours. So, if I really want to do something, if there is a dream that I would like to pursue, then I will have to find a way of fitting it into those 24 hours. The truth is, even though I complain about not having enough time to spend on the things that I would like to do, I am embarrassed to admit the amount of time that I spend scrolling aimlessly through social media platforms. I convince myself that that is my way of relaxing. I fail to realize that there is an energy that is required to engage in anything. That there is an energy that I exchange through any form of active or inactive interaction.

No one is going to hand me success. No one is going to give me a break. The bills will not pay themselves. Neither is anyone going to pursue my dreams for me. Even as a student, Ronke had a routine that she followed. She went to bed at 9pm and woke up at 5am. Between 5am and 7am, she would take a shower, say her prayers, check and respond to emails and have breakfast. She would then work until about 1pm when she would take her lunch break. At 2pm she resumed work and finished at 5pm, after which she would watch episodes of *Friends* and other entertainment. She would then make her dinner. She liked having people around so when she could, she had dinner with friends. Our weekends were spent eating cake, watching movies and hanging around in malls.

They say you eat an elephant bit by bit. It starts with saying: "If this is what I want to achieve five years down the road, every day, I will put aside an hour or half an hour to work towards this dream. I will learn more about this thing. I will schedule some time to talk to people who know about this thing. I will start. And I will be consistent." If the dream is to write children's books, how about starting by reading a children's book every night? If you are thinking of starting a business, what networking events are you attending? What YouTube videos are you watching to learn more about the business? Do you spend a little time every day (even thirty minutes) learning? How much money are you putting away every month to save for your business?

The reality is, for most of us, it is difficult to wake up one day and walk out of our jobs to pursue our dreams. So, we need to bite the elephant bit by bit.

KEEPING WITH YOUR JOURNEY… AND ASKING FOR HELP ALONG THE WAY

SOMETIME IN 2017, I went to a workshop in Arusha, Tanzania. While casually chatting with one of the workshop participants, I found out that she and a few others went for a run every morning at 6am. I am not a jogger. And at the time, I was terrified of dogs (I am still afraid of dogs, but a few friends are helping me get over the fear). One morning, I decided to join the joggers. I was aware of the fact that part of the route that they took had stray dogs. I was also aware of the fact that I was going to be much slower than most of my new friends, who were seasoned joggers. I did not want to slow them down. But I knew that I needed to listen to my body. And so, every time I started racing in order to catch up with them, I would remind myself: "Listen to your body, Jalia". And I would slow down.

There was, however, one main problem with listening to my body. If I stayed too far behind, what would happen if a dog appeared out of the blue and there was no one in sight to help me?

Something seemingly simple, yet profound, happened. Even though my new friends (who I had only known for a couple of days) were jogging way ahead of me, every time they came across a dog, two of them would come jogging back to where I was to make sure that I felt safe. The rest of the group would wait ahead. This happened at least five times in the one hour that we jogged.

It got me thinking about life more generally. It was a reminder that I should travel at my pace without feeling the need to race against or catch up with others. It was a reminder that I should stick with my truth. More profoundly, it was a reminder that when you let people know the challenges that you face, when you ask people for help, there will be people who are willing to step in and offer help. It was also a reminder that not everyone is interested in getting there first and fast. For some people, the satisfaction comes from knowing that they helped another person get there too, even when that may mean slowing down their own journey.

"Nze Ani?" ... "Who Am I?"

THE BAGANDA HAVE AN expression: *nze ani?* Literally translated, it means "Who am I?" The expression is often used to register disbelief at one's unexpected fortune. For example, an economically impoverished man may ask (while putting his hand on his chest and lowering his head in a bow) *"nze ani?"* when, at his daughter's wedding, there are dignitaries among the guests. Who is he, a poor man, to attract all these rich and powerful people to his homestead?

The expression is normally intended as a twin symbol of humility and gratitude. And yet it can also serve as a form of belittling oneself. Who am I to receive all that praise? Who am I to attain that level of success? Who am I to even dream of greatness? Really, *nze ani?*

In 2016, I started posting daily gratitude posts on my Facebook wall. This was followed with weekly random musings in 2017. My Facebook friends started paying more attention to the things that I was saying. A number of friends encouraged me to write a book. One of my friends referred to me as the Ugandan Chimamanda Ngozi Adichie, a writer I greatly admire. Another suggested that I should give a TED talk. And another suggested that I should submit one of my musings as an article to the Huffington Post. I started to panic. My internal critic was active: "*Nze ani*?" "I am nowhere near as good a writer as Chimamanda Ngozi Adichie. Have these people actually read Chimamanda's books? Have they read Maya Angelou?" "They are just being kind. That is what friends do." "Apart from my siblings and a few friends, who will even buy a book that I write?" "*Nze ani*?"

The thing about *nze ani* is that it diminishes our capabilities in two respects. First, it enlarges others. Second, it reduces or flattens us. Speaking about Martin Luther King in a 1990 interview with the Academy of Achievement, Maya Angelou said:

> It is very dangerous to make a person larger than life. Because then, young men and women are tempted to believe, 'Well, if he was THAT great, he's inaccessible and I can never try to be that or emulate that or achieve that.' The truth is, Martin Luther King was a human being.

Nze ani creates a thick and impenetrable divide between us and those that we look up to. It makes them unreachable. Inaccessible. We dwarf ourselves and our abilities. We start to think that our thinking does not matter. That our stories are not important. That our ideas have no value. Equally dangerous, *nze ani* gives its utterer an excuse not to try. And when you do try, an excuse for mediocrity. After all, we think, *I can never attain that level of brilliance. I can never write as well as that person. I can never debate as well as that person. The design of my cakes cannot get to the level of that person's. I can never do the back bend or headstand the way that person does it. I can never sing like that person. I can never reach that level of spirituality.* When we decide that it is unfathomable to stand on the same stage with "those people" we fail to put in the work that is required to get us to where we aspire to be. We continue dreaming and hoping that one day, magically, the dream will turn itself into a reality.

There is, of course, the opposite of *nze ani*, which in this day and age is *nzuno* (here I am). We are in such a rush to prove that we are great and that we have figured things out. We want instant gratification. We want to become overnight successes. Social media has, of course, intensified this pressure. There is pressure to say something all the time, to put out a video right now, "before people forget about me!" People share things that they have not even verified, just because they want to be the first to post. *The bus is leaving! I must make my point now or I will have no point! I will be no more!*

Both *nze ani* and *nzuno* are cries for approval. Waiting or calling on others to endorse us. Needing permission from others to do the things that we want to do. To decide for us who we can be and who we should be. We forget that we are all human and we all have human ingredients.

Instead of paralyzing ourselves with *nze ani* or overwhelming ourselves with *nzuno*, perhaps we should ask ourselves: what do I need to do to get to where I want to be? And then breathe and start the journey, step by step. Bit by bit.

"The Thesis Will Not Write Itself "

MANY YEARS AGO, WHEN I was struggling to complete my PhD thesis and coming up with all kinds of excuses about why I was not making progress, my sister-friend, Mosope, told me: "The thesis will not write itself." Like many graduate students, I had mastered the art of procrastination. I would attend endless conferences. I would join reading groups to read anything so that I did not have to write. I would offer to read other people's work because that often meant that I did not have to do my own work. I would go to the mall. I would go hiking. And swimming. I would attend endless potlucks. And then I would cry out in frustration about the fact that I was not making much progress on my thesis and that the ideas were just not flowing. And Mosope said, "The thesis will not write itself. You need to write. Whatever comes into your head. Just write."

Many years later, I watched Mel Robbins, who is famously known for her five-second rule. Mel concludes that decisions are often made in five-second windows. She emphasizes the need for action, even when we don't feel like it. In fact, particularly when we don't feel like it. Because, she argues, the problem is that we have been sold the idea that motivation will come raining down on us. That we shall just be sitting there one day and then have that "aha" moment, which will connect us to our divine purpose and propel us into action. The reality, she argues, is quite different. The reality is that we have to act. We have to get up. We have to decide to do. We have to move, even when we don't feel like it. "The thesis will not write itself."

We often think that for the things that we love to do, motivation will simply give birth to itself. That all we need to do is to wait for that moment when we are inspired. I remember the time when Annette and I started talking about this book. I was still in full-time employment. I was very excited about the idea and decided that every now and then, I would use my annual leave to write the book. I called it my "bookation". I remember the first time I took my *bookation*. The first day of my annual leave was a Friday. I looked forward to sitting down and just pouring my heart out, typing away. My head was saturated with brilliant ideas. And then Friday came. Nothing. No wisdom. No inspiration. I thought that I would jump out of bed like batwoman; instead, I crawled. Every brilliant idea that I had in my head before that Friday now sounded so lame when I tried to put it on paper. "This is just not the right moment," I told myself, "I will wait until tomorrow or in the middle of the night when my creative juices begin to flow." I shut down the laptop. That night, there was nothing. Neither was there much the next morning.

I was distraught. Did this mean that my ideas were not as exciting as I had imagined them to be? If they didn't excite me, how did I expect them to excite my readers? Did this mean that I was not a writer?

I remembered Mosope's words: "The thesis will not write itself."

On Day Three of my *bookation*, I decided to write – even though I didn't feel like writing. Still, nothing inspiring. But I wrote anyway. The same thing happened on Day Four. And then on Day Five, something started happening. I started smiling at some of the words that were appearing before me. I started laughing at some of the expressions that I had come up with. I didn't like everything, but I liked some things. And soon, I started really liking many things!

Not all the days of writing were the same. I had some really good days and some terrible days. But if I had waited for inspiration to come raining down on me, I would probably still be here – two years later – writing the book beautifully in my head but having nothing on paper to show for it.

I have learnt that whatever it is that I desire to do, whatever it is that I dream of, it is important that I do not romanticize the process of achieving it. It is important that I do not wait for motivation to come raining down on me. What I need to do instead is to start. And keep moving … even when I don't feel like it. Somewhere

along the way, I meet with inspiration and we comple-
ment each other. This has been the case whether I am
trying to write something or I am going on my morning
walks or I need to make a decision about something.

Now that I think about it, "The thesis will not write
itself" makes me think of my mother. My mother is one
of the smartest entrepreneurs that I know. She did not
have much of a formal education, but she certainly has a
brilliant business mind. In 1994, she opened up a fast-food
restaurant, Tipsy TakeAway, with very little capital. Every
night, she would come home with a small envelope filled
with notes and coins. My siblings and I would go into her
bedroom to count the money that she had made at work
that day. I remember when we counted the first 100,000
Uganda shillings (approximately twenty-seven US dollars
in today's currency). It seemed like we were counting non-
stop! We could not believe it when we set up the piles of
notes on one side and added them to the coins and they
added up to 100,000 shillings! That weekend, Mum took
us for ice cream to celebrate the milestone.

As a single mother, her daily prayer was that she would
live long enough to see all her children complete school.
Her dream and prayer for Tipsy was that it would provide
us with enough income so that she would not be worried
about things like school fees and food. Thankfully, she
had inherited a house in a decent neighbourhood from
her father, which we lived in, so at least we did not have
to worry about rent. Over the years, Tipsy became two
things: a small business and a big business. It was a small
business in the sense that it was a family-owned busi-

ness which relied primarily on modest family-injected capital. It was a big business in the sense that it gave our mother purpose and a livelihood. It fuelled her passion and fed her soul. It schooled us – her biological children and other children – both in the literal sense and in the ways of the world (we worked there during school holidays). But mostly, what made Tipsy big was that it was not just about us. It was also about the various people that it employed over the years. Many of these people were unskilled workers who had a hard time finding employment. Because of Tipsy, they were able to feed their families, to send their children to school and to access healthcare. Because of Tipsy, they could afford to dream. Tipsy gave them a sense of purpose, a place that they could call home. Most importantly, it gave them a sense of pride and dignity. They woke up every morning having a place to go to.

One person in particular stands out. We call him "Boyi". As the name suggests, Boyi was quite young when he knocked on the doors of Tipsy looking for a job. He was willing to do anything. He didn't know much about cooking, but he wanted to earn a living. He said he could mop the floors and do general cleaning. My mother offered him the job immediately. Boyi was at work by 5.30 in the morning, mopping the floors and earning a daily wage. However, he was also curious and eager to learn. He befriended the head chef, Kibirige, who used to make the chaps (a kind of mince pattie) and liver that Tipsy became famous for. Every time Boyi finished his work, he would go and watch Kibirige.

One day, Kibirige fell ill and there was no one to make the chaps and liver – Tipsy's hottest selling products. We were stuck. Boyi said that he knew how to make them, and my mother had no choice but to take his word for it. He made such amazing chaps that he was immediately promoted.

Twenty-seven years later, Boyi is still with Tipsy as one of the top chefs. He has a magic touch. Whether he is making grilled chicken or pilau rice, if Boyi is the one who has made the dish, it will have his Midas touch.

A few years ago, the Kampala City Council Authority demolished buildings in Wandegeya, where Tipsy is located. Tipsy was terribly affected. It was already a difficult economic environment. Many people in business were struggling and Tipsy was no exception. We were worried about what the demolition would mean for Tipsy's continuity. We were particularly worried about how this would affect our mother. Tipsy was, after all, her baby, her home, her joy. But there was something else that we were worried about. We – our mother and her children – would not be as negatively affected as the people who worked at Tipsy. My siblings and I all had sources of income that were independent of Tipsy. But we were worried about the employees and what this would mean for them.

My mother and my younger brother, Moses, had already started preparing another location for Tipsy in Wandegeya for when the inevitable demolition would happen. However, they had hoped that we still

had another six months or so before the demolition. I
remember that Friday afternoon when the city council
put a padlock on the doors of Tipsy and other businesses
in Wandegeya. I remember my sister, Sarah, and I going
to the city council to request that they should give us
some time as a community, to prepare. The answer was
no. Moses, being a perfectionist, wanted everything to
be impeccable before the new Tipsy opened its doors
to the public. My mother, on the other hand, being a
realist and a doer, believed that things did not have to
be perfect. So, to Moses's horror, she said that we would
open up the new Tipsy the next evening (Saturday),
whether or not we were ready. As long as health and
safety had been taken into account, she said, we would
just have to work with what we had. She wanted Tipsy's loyal customers to know that we were still there to
serve them.

She went into the city, bought a few potted plants to
make the place look pretty, and told some Tipsy workers
to turn up early the next morning. She asked someone
to handwrite a poster that we would place on the locked
door to let customers know where we had moved to.
Two workers would also be physically stationed there
to direct – and if need be, accompany – customers to
the new site.

The next evening, we opened the doors of the new
Tipsy and in old family tradition, each of my mother's
children who was in town turned up to work alongside
the Tipsy staff. Obviously, Boyi was there too, beaming
with excitement. Our customers did not disappoint: They

turned up in huge numbers. And at the end of the night, just like we had done over two decades ago, we went back home with Mum to talk about how the evening had gone. This time, we did not count money. We were counting our collective memories of a magical night.

Forty and Not
Fabulous

I HAD A GRAND plan. I was going to be forty and absolutely fabulous. To be sure to achieve my goal, I would
start seriously embarking on the plan a year before my
fortieth birthday. I was going to be in perfect shape. I
was going to drink so much water, eat so little junk food,
reduce on the dosage of my chocolate intake, and have just
enough facials to make my skin glow like those gorgeous
women on the cover of Vogue. But what is beauty without
brains, you may ask? Well, I had that part covered too.
By the time I clocked forty, I would have published two
books. We would be living in our own home (because my
published books would have been bestsellers). I would be
on track to true financial independence. Also, obviously,
I would be wiser, more poised and more graceful. Forty
would be my year. Because is this not the year that most
women point to as their year of liberation? Well, I too,
would come into my womanhood.

Tick tock. Tick tock. Tick tock.

May 2018. Forty at last!

But alas ... not quite feeling the fabulosity. My face was on rampage, having been attacked by something that I am still trying to figure out to this day. My intimate relationship with chocolate and constant flirtation with almond croissants meant that I was nowhere near my ideal weight (it doesn't matter whether you eat these things in the dark or in broad daylight. Hips don't lie. True story). I hadn't published any book (boooohoooo!) And I was still making enough mistakes to remind me that I had a long way to go on my journey to Wiseland. To put it bluntly, on that day of declared fabulosity, I was feeling kind of old but far from fabulous. While I would not go as far as saying that I was miserable, there was a lot on my inside that was still crying. And even though I was surrounded with love and I greatly appreciated that love, there was still some lingering internal emptiness. I felt under accomplished. I began to get frustrated and impatient with the fact that I had made such little progress achieving my goals. ... Okay, so maybe I was a little miserable.

I started nibbling on some questions. Is forty really what it is made out to be? Do women really feel more fabulous, more sexy, more composed, more in tune with their emotions and more accomplished when they clock forty? Have we, by that age, really figured out how to throw out all the garbage from the past and not pay attention to unsolicited opinions? Is forty really the year of liberation and reinvention? Why forty? Why not thirty-four or fifty-six or sixty-two? Who created this standard? What do we miss in the process of working towards achieving certain goals by certain due dates? Does having aspirations for the future mean that we do not enjoy the now, which is the most certain present? And who are we comparing ourselves with? What is their story? What is their history? What is their future?

I think ambition is important. I think vision helps with perspective. And I think plans are necessary to breathe life into ambitions and vision. But I also think that when we focus too much on what we could be and what we need to achieve by a certain date, we deny ourselves what we are and what we have in the present. When we dwell so much on what we will have – whether it be money or body or fame – in the future, we fail to appreciate and treasure all the other things that we do have now. When we are obsessed with an image that right now appears to be beyond our reach, we spend our time chasing after shadows of happiness when we could in fact immerse ourselves in the beauty of the reality that currently defines our existence. Like being able to breathe without assistance. Or see. Or walk. Or have family and friends. Or have food in our refrigerator and a roof over our heads. When we create images about how much better life on the other side is, we devalue the progress that we have made to get to where we are. But mostly, when we compare with the misguided illusion that we shall achieve what another person has by a certain age, we leave ourselves vulnerable to a tasteless existence and susceptible to chronic dissatisfaction.

A couple of weeks later, I declared: I am forty. I am fabulous. And I am going to have some (more) chocolate.

WOMEN FOR WOMEN

"Agali awamu gegaluma enyama."
"Teeth that are closer together are more effective at
biting meat than those that are apart."

~ *Kiganda proverb*

IT IS QUITE COMMON to hear people say that women
do not wish each other well. Or that women make
things unnecessarily difficult for fellow women. At the
same time, it is increasingly common to witness and
hear of cases of women supporting each other, cheering
each other on and speaking up for each other. Women
in leadership positions mentoring younger women.
Mothers-in-law speaking up for daughters-in-law. White
women allying with Black women in the fight against
racism.

There appears to be more evidence of "women for
women". Still, I sometimes wonder: what does women
for women really mean?

At the 2016 Women in the World Summit, held in
New York City, one of my favourite world leaders, Indra

Nooyi (the former CEO of PepsiCo) talked about how, frequently, women fail to help each other out in the workplace. She gave examples of how women compete with each other in workplaces and how, often, women prefer male colleagues over female ones. The example that struck me the most was the one where she compared the different ways in which men and women give and receive feedback. She gave the example of Bill, who gives a presentation that is not going well. During the break, the conversation in the men's washroom goes something like:

"Hey Bill. Your presentation is awful. Fix it, man."

His male colleagues give him tips on how to improve his presentation. Bill goes back and the second half of the presentation is superb. Indra said that in contrast, when a woman receives the same feedback from a fellow woman, she thinks to herself:

"God! She's so bitchy!"

Or worse, her female colleagues – either not wanting to hurt her feelings or secretly celebrating her shortcomings – are not candid about her presentation. Indra concludes:

> We assume that feedback from fellow women means something is wrong. But if that same feedback came to us from men, we're willing to accept it. Or worse still, we don't give the feedback to women the way we should. Even though we know that they're not doing well because, we go, 'Good, she's struggling. I can take her position'.

Indra's observations challenge me to ask myself the following questions:

How do I provide feedback to fellow women? Am I able to criticize the act without attacking the person?

How do I receive and act on feedback from fellow women?

Am I courageous enough to tell my female friends uncomfortable truths and to ask them tough questions?

Do I take every opportunity that I get to shine a bright light on the accomplishments of another woman?

Do I feel threatened by the success of a fellow woman or do I draw inspiration from it?

Do I elevate myself in judgement of other women or do I reach out to embrace them?

When a fellow woman honours me by confiding in me about her struggles, do I treasure this honour and feel blessed that she has chosen to trust me with her story, or do I instead feel superior to her?

Do I belong to a women's circle? How do I hold space for other women in my circle?

How do I use my positions of privilege to make space for other women at the table?

And, perhaps most importantly, do I, to borrow Jean Houston's expression, practise "radical empathy" towards fellow women? Am I able to see myself in other women?

I Am Her. And I Can No Longer Contain the Silence.

Her name is Stella
She is loud
And utters obscenities
Nothing really like me
For I am prim
And proper
Polite
And politically correct.
When you locked her up in prison
I kept silent
But then I looked at my children
And wondered
What would it feel like
If I was taken away from the gifts of my womb?

Her name is Aisha
When you took her husband away

Claiming that he was a suspect
In a crime of murder
I was silent
But later
You came for her
And then went for her children
Mother, children and father
Separated
And I thought to myself
What would I do
If my children were taken away from me?

They call her Maama Tina
A single mother
She used to sell *kabalagala*
And fried *muwogo*
On the dusty streets of Kampala
Until you set up
A "modern market"
And demanded that she pays fees
To get a stall in the "modern market".
Maama Tina
She no longer sells her *kabalagala*
And her *muwogo*
She cannot afford the market fees
She doesn't know
What her children will eat tomorrow
Let alone today
What would I do
If I couldn't afford to feed my children?

Still, I remained silent.

I remained silent
Because
I feared to suffer similar consequences
I remained silent
Because
I was afraid of being political
I remained silent
Because
I was not directly affected.

But my silence is no longer plausible
It is punctuated
With huge exclamations of betrayal
My silence is no longer comfortable
It sits like heavy metal
At the pit of my stomach
My silence is no longer politically correct
It is an obscenity.

The mother in me is encumbered
With guilt and with shame
I can no longer look at my children
Without wondering about their children
The political
Has become quite personal

I am a woman

A mother
A wife
A daughter
I am Stella
I am Aisha
I am Maama Tina
And until you give them their freedom
My own freedom will remain an illusion
Until you return their livelihood
Mine will be a borrowed livelihood.

I am her
And I can no longer contain the silence.

HOW CAN WE
CREATE HEALING
THROUGH OUR WORDS?

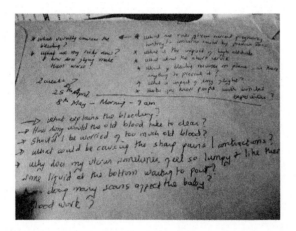

As I LOOKED AT the thick clots of blood dripping into the toilet, I had two thoughts. The first one was: "Not another miscarriage. Please God. I cannot handle another miscarriage." The second thought, which was even more scary, had been planted in me by the stern warning of a renowned gynaecologist in Uganda. A year before this incident, she had told me: "If you do not take out that particular fibroid, it will be extremely difficult for you to conceive. And if you do conceive, you will definitely miscarry."

"... you will definitely miscarry."

"... you will definitely miscarry."

It was the conviction and finality with which she uttered those words that now haunted me and would haunt me for the next two and a half months. They were the words of an expert. But they were also the words of a woman, who herself had once carried a child. They had not been minced. And every time blood showed up in my urine – or instead of urine (because, despite pleas from my dear cousin, Shidah, not to do so, I did look every time I went to the toilet) – those words scolded me.

A few months later, when the bleeding had stopped, I was scheduled to travel back to Canada. But before I could do so, I needed some reassurance from a doctor that it would be safe to travel. By that time, for various reasons, we had already moved through three doctors. I explained to the fourth doctor, a woman in her late fifties or early sixties, that I needed to travel, but only if it was safe for me and the little human that was kicking inside me.

I will never forget her words: "What do you want? The child or to travel?"

I was confused. And so she explained. After reminding me of how turbulent my pregnancy had been, she reminded me of the little fact that I was no longer a young woman (I was 35). What if, she asked, this was my last chance to have a child? Did I want the child, or did I want to travel?

Once again, there was no mincing of words. I was being scolded. Maybe even threatened.

When my mother and I walked out of that hospital, we were both livid. I was in physical and emotional pain. How could these doctors, fellow women, not see this?

We moved to the next doctor – number five. He was a much younger gynaecologist who had been recommended by my dear friend Jackie. Unlike the previous doctors, Dr Emmanuel was not offended by my many questions, which had been nervously and frantically scribbled on both sides of an A4 brown envelop over the course of my several doctors' visits (see picture at the beginning of the chapter). He did not perceive the questions as challenging his authority or doubting his judgement. He seemed to understand my vulnerability. He seemed to know that more than anything, what I needed was reassurance – or at least an explanation that was not intended to shut me up or blame me any more than I was already blaming myself. He answered each of my questions patiently and thoughtfully. "No, the scans will not hurt your baby, but we shall limit them." "We do not know the cause of the bleeding. No, it is not definitely because of the fibroid." "You may be able to travel back to Canada. But let us monitor your situation for the next four to six weeks and see." We came up with a plan. We would not be making any concrete decisions at this point in time. We would play it by ear. If at six and a half months there were no high risks, I could travel. Dr. Emmanueal did not make any promises. And yet for the first time in months, I walked away with a glimmer of hope. For the first time, I felt that someone was seeing me and listening to my pain. For the first time, I felt like I was healing. For the first time, I could picture myself holding my baby in my arms. And three months later, I did.

We are normally told that a patient's healing is tied to their attitude. Their willingness to fight. We also know that this attitude is influenced by various things. It could be their religious faith, it could be their internal strength, and it could be the bedside manner of a doctor who is patient and willing to address what may seem like silly questions. A doctor who empathizes with a patient's emotions and recognizes their vulnerability. A doctor who remembers that as much as other people have gone through similar experiences, at that moment, that experience is unique to the patient before them. Their suffering is real. And that the doctor's words have the ability to take some of that pain away or pile on it.

These two doctors, who happened to be female, had options. They could have chosen to encourage me. Instead, they chose to threaten me. They could have chosen to give me hope. Instead, they burdened me with guilt. They could have held my hand and said that they knew that the options that they were giving me were tough but that we would somehow figure this out together. Instead, they pointed fingers at me and scolded me. They bashed me, as if I was not already feeling battered.

They forgot that I was a human being going through a very human experience.

They forgot to give birth with me.

KIM BROOKS

I WAS A TIMID African student in a foreign country. Aside from the fact that it felt like it was minus fifty degrees outside, I was shivering from the shock of what I had just got myself into. What had I been thinking, signing up for a Master's degree in a country that was miles and flights away from home, weather that was so foreign to my Black skin and technology that was so removed from my comfort zone (those who know me know that I have a special relationship with technology)? As I walked into Professor Kim Brooks's office that morning, pen and notebook purposely held in my hand (I could at least look serious to make up for my want of confidence), I questioned again what I had been thinking when I had got myself into this scary mess.

There, I met a lady looking much younger than I had expected. "Hi, I am Kim!" she said, cheerfully. "I will be your supervisor. I don't know much about taxation in Africa. But I know something about tax more generally." She then went ahead to tell me about her area of work and asked if I had any questions. My meekness rendered me mute.

At the end of the meeting, she said, "Oh, one more thing. If at any point in time you feel that I am not giving you the support that you need, please let me know. Also, there are professors X and Y who are experts in tax. If at any time you feel that they would be better supervisors, don't be afraid to let me know. The most important thing is that you enjoy this journey and that you work with someone that you are comfortable with."

There is a reason why Kim Brooks has won teaching excellence awards in almost every university that she has taught. Kim is not just passionate about tax. She also cares deeply about people. And she promotes and boosts the morale of people, particularly her students. When I was a graduate student, Kim would take me with her to conferences filled with professors (even during my PhD when I was not under her supervision). On a number of occasions, I was the only student in these meetings. Kim would introduce me to the other professors: "You all need to listen to the amazing work that Jalia is doing!" she would announce cheerfully. "Can you believe she has managed to do X, Y and Z? I don't know how she does it but she's just fantastic!" The other professors would look at me with renewed interest. If we were working jointly on a project, she would let me be the one to make the presentation.

Kim made me believe that I might actually be fantastic!

I often don't take academics to my mother's home because they either tend to engage in dense conversa-

tions, which exclude the everyday person, or they have
an awkward existential presence, which makes them
somewhat incapable of surviving outside the walls of
their faculty buildings. But when Kim visited Uganda
for work, I did not think twice about taking her home. I
had seen how she connected with people from different
walks of life. When she got there, she ate *matooke* (green
bananas) and *kinyebwa* (peanut paste) like she had been
raised in the Ugandan village of Butambala. She joked
about wanting to move into my mother's house when
my elder sister, Sarah, who was soon getting married,
moved out.

Like many African mothers, my mother gets ani-
mated when people visit. Even more when they express
an appreciation for her culinary skills. By the end of the
day, my mother was so excited that she was even giving
out things that did not belong to her! She gave Kim a
colourful handwoven mat. Kim, in her effortless and
instinctive connection with cultural differences, immediately humoured her by getting off the chair and sitting
on the mat, like a proper Muganda girl. And then she
looked up at the sun and said she wished she could stay
there forever and not have to go back to Canada. Mother
was so happy! She put her hand on her chest and told
Kim, "You make me so happy!", to which Kim replied,
"You make me so happy too!"

Over the years, Kim has taught me a number of things.

My voice matters. She taught me that I might not be
using the kind of sophisticated language that often per-
meates academic circles, but that did not mean that I did

not have something important to say. I try to remember this every time I get nervous about speaking in public.

Humility – it came as a great shock to me for a professor to confess during our first meeting that she did not know. She went ahead to say that while she would do a great job of guiding me on how to think about my thesis, we needed a specialist – preferably an African – who properly understood how taxes worked in the African context. It was through this process that I connected with Seth Terkper, then an International Monetary Fund economist, who turned out to be a great mentor. Kim taught me that it was okay to say, "I don't know." That this did not mean that I was less competent – it just meant that I knew enough to know that I did not know everything.

Connection: Kim's instant connection with my mother showed me what happens when we freely allow our hearts to meet. When the only agenda that we have is to find connection.

The Table of Life

Today I sat at the table of experience
Nibbling on wisdom
Aged forty to sixty-nine

Today I listened to courageous women
Whose stories rejuvenated me
Whose vulnerability vaccinated my anxiety
Whose compassion emboldened me

Today I sat at the foot of wisdom
Marinated in years of gracefulness
Held together by resilience
And acceptance

Today I was a student
In lessons of life
Of women
Who dared to love and to let go
Who embraced pain
And reserved a seat for uncertainty

Today I was comforted
With the knowledge that
Mistakes will not extinguish me
Pain may visit
But need not stay
And that even at the murmur of seventy
New dreams can be birthed

Today
On this table of life
I travelled from England through Ireland
Celebrated Pakistan
And honoured Bosnia
Deepened my roots in Uganda
All the time being reminded
That we are one
Separated only by time
And sometimes space
But connected
Through spirit

Today I was humbled
I was inspired
Reminded to slow down
I was cherished
For my humanity
And my womanhood
At the table of life.

GRATITUDE AND PRAYER

I AM GRATEFUL TO be alive to be writing this. I have been favoured with good health. I have eyes that see, ears that hear, limbs that function and a brain, which – even with its occasional freezing – still serves me well. For all of these, I say, *Alhamdullilah*, "Thank you God". I am grateful.

As I write this, I hear sounds of little children in the next room. They are my daughters. They are loud and they are full of life. I am grateful.

I am grateful for my husband. His calmness. His patience. His wisdom. And his friendship.

I am grateful for the precious gift of family, particularly my mother, my sisters and my brothers. They are a constant in my life. They are present, even when they are not nearby. They love me, even when we disagree.

I am grateful for my many friendships. Some quite old, others relatively new. All very precious. They have taught me, they have comforted me, they have brought me great joy.

I am grateful to have a source of income, even an inconsistent one.

I pray for those who are standing by the bedsides of their loved ones or waiting by the phone, hoping that they will make it through the next minute, the next hour, the next day, the next month. May God bring them healing and miracles.

I pray for the mother, father or carer who does not have a source of income. Who wonders where the next meal is going to come from. I pray for the person who has been rendered homeless because they have lost their source of income. The one who has lost their home to wars or fires or debt or natural disasters. The little boy or little girl whose parents have been taken away.

I pray for peace. In our homes. In our places of work. In our neighbourhoods. In our countries. In the depths of our hearts.

I pray that we use our words to build, not to break. That our tongues are not used to curtail the spirits of others. That we learn to speak with each other instead of past each other. That we look at each other as we speak and we listen to the words that are coming out of each other's mouths.

I pray that we are more awake and more kind to our environment. That we are more present in the lives of those that matter the most to us. And that we are grateful for small fortunes and take great pleasure in the simple things.

I pray that we learn to be more tolerant of those who are different from us. That we celebrate the wins of others in a manner similar to how we would our own, and that we mourn their losses as if they had visited us.

I pray that we are more patient with our young ones and more kind to our elderly.

I pray that we gain the courage to live out our values, speak up for what is right and pursue our wildest dreams.

Lastly, I pray that we develop the habit of being more mindful of our actions, more generous with our praise, more careful with our words and more grateful for the things that we have and the things that we are getting right, even as we acknowledge the work we still need to do.

A Woman's Manifesto

I AM BEAUTIFUL. I am intelligent. I am blessed.

I will develop the courage to fall in love with myself. To laugh at myself when I make mistakes. And to forgive myself when I mess up.

I will love my body. This powerhouse that hosts this beautiful soul. The vessel that transports me through life. I will love its dimples and its scars.

I will speak kindly to myself. Serve myself with portions of compassion similar to those that I give out to others.

I will embrace my femininity to the fullest. I will cry when I feel pain and when I feel joy. I will seek help when I feel burdened. I will learn to say "I am not okay" when I am not okay.

I will not wait to be rescued. I am the captain of my ship.

I will invite joy into my heart and abundance into my life.

I will protect my mental space. I will keep out toxic thoughts and toxic people. I will say no to endless demands on my time. And I will surround myself with doers and dreamers.

When I start to hear those whispers that tell me that "I am not good enough", "I am not intelligent enough", "I am not beautiful enough", I will throw my head back and smile. Breathe in and say, "Oh, fake news. Fake news. I understand you want an audience. Sorry. Not me. I am too busy being fabulous."

I will love fellow women fiercely. I will celebrate their victories. I will empathize with their pain. I will hug them tightly and sit with them silently through their pain. I will remember that they are me and I am them.

I will belong to a nest. A circle of women who will remind me of who I am when I become deluded. Women with whom I will share stories and break bread. Women who will cry with me and make me laugh. Women who will challenge me and inspire me.

I will listen to the songs of birds, accept the tears of children and surrender to the will of God.

I will resist the temptation to control. To try and control the outcomes of my actions. To try and control the actions of my man. To try and control the footsteps of my children.

I will speak my truth even when it makes others uncomfortable. I will speak my truth, not just for me, but also to lend my voice to those who may not be in position to speak.

I will plant a seed. A rose. A pumpkin. An idea. And I will water it patiently and diligently, knowing that when its time comes, it will blossom.

I will eat good chocolate and taste its deliciousness. I will feel its sweetness at the basement of my stomach. But I will not use chocolate to numb my pain. I will not use chocolate to run away from my problems. And I will certainly not use chocolate to fill an emotional void.

I will keep trying even when I keep falling.

I will resist the urge to judge, the temptation to belittle and the desire to compete. Instead, I will be curious. I will seek motivation. And I will ask questions.

I will not participate in any mission intended to drag another woman through the mud. Indeed, I will not be part of any derogatory mission, whoever its target be.

I will not make it my business to try and understand the complex machinations of people's minds. I will remind myself that I am not a psychologist.

I will receive God's love fully.

I will embrace each new year of age with grace, without giving up my youthful playfulness.

I will dare to love and fall in love, remembering always to reserve enough love for myself.

I will give myself permission to stop. To take a break. To change direction. To do nothing. To sit still. To honour the murmurs of my heart.

I will laugh until I cry. Love until I die. Search until I find.

I will read a book. Sing a song. Dance to the beats of drums. Tell stories. I will not die with my music in me.

Luganda-English Glossary

akso .... accent (slang)
dole ze byaayi .... dolls made out of banana fibre
Ffe tuli embata ento .... We are little ducks (a nursery rhyme)
gomesi .... traditional Ugandan outfit for women
guma .... be strong
kabalagala .... a local pancake
kalo .... millet meal
kinyebwa .... peanut paste
koja .... uncle
kukyaala .... a meeting of the families of a bride and groom before their marriage
kusiba sumbusa .... making a face
kwanjula .... introduction/marriage ceremony
kwepena .... the equivalent of dodgeball, normally played by young children
matooke .... green bananas
mwami .... husband
meketu .... a hard corn delicacy

mukyala gundi.. someone's wife
muwogo ....cassava
nyama choma.. roasted meat
nze ani?...who am I?
nzuno..here I am
okutambula kwekumanya.................. to travel is to learn
ssenga...paternal aunt
sukuma wiki ....a type of kale
taata.. father
tapo ....the equivalent of hide and seek
ugali...cornmeal

About the Authors

Jalia Kangave

JALIA KANGAVE IS THE author of *Love Notes to a Dear Daughter*, a collection of bitesize pieces of advice to young ladies, particularly in their teenage years. When she is not trying to keep up with her two energetic daughters, she is experiencing and reflecting on the multiple layers of womanhood - whether it is in her academic research on the gender dimensions of taxation, her personal life as a mother and wife, her mentoring of young female professionals or her everyday interactions with mums on playgrounds and school gates. Jalia loves spending time in the company of women, taking long solo walks, wearing African print fabric and delighting in chocolate. She lives in Brighton, United Kingdom with her husband and two daughters.

Annette Tush

FROM A TENDER AGE, Annette Tush always wondered about what her purpose in life was. Following the death of her one- year-old daughter, she relocated from Uganda to Canada, finally settling in the USA where she resides with her husband and three lovely boys. After years of battling with so many "why" questions, her purpose in life has become crystal clear. Annette feels truly blessed, even though, like most people, she has not been spared from dark seasons. It is events such as the premature death of her only daughter, which almost shuttered her life, that have become the cornerstones of her life's purpose and inspired her to inspire others to laugh more, forgive more and soar above life's misfortunes.

Printed in Great Britain
by Amazon